WHEN THE LAMP FLICKERS

WHEN THE LAMP FLICKERS

Leslie D. Weatherhead

"Thy word is a lamp unto my feet, and a light unto my path."—Ps. 119:105

ABINGDON-COKESBURY PRESS
NEW YORK • NASHVILLE

WHEN THE LAMP FLICKERS

B

SET UP, PRINTED, AND BOUND BY THE PARTHENON PRESS AT NASHVILLE, TENNESSEE, UNITED STATES OF AMERICA

This book is gratefully dedicated to
the councilors, officers, members, and congregation
of
THE CITY TEMPLE
London

who through twelve difficult years, driven by war to worship successively in seven different buildings, have given me prayerful affection, loyal support, and unrestricted freedom to do the work of the Christian ministry

Preface

It has become increasingly plain that religion as at present organized is not reaching the great masses of our people. To put it bluntly, our services are not well attended. I shall not here attempt to diagnose this situation or apportion blame. We have had many diagnoses, but few suggested remedies. And blaming people for not going to church, or parsons for not ministering adequately to them when they do go, is certainly not a job I am fit to do.

At the City Temple we have, however, tried an interesting experiment. We realized that part of our service was quite boring, and often unintelligible, to the man on the fringe of religion. He is interested in what Christianity has to say, but our prayers are often couched in language that leaves him out of it, and our hymns he often hates. The sentiment of them *is* sometimes rather sickly, and, in any case, he has not got to the point where he can use such language. Even Charles Wesley's great hymns, he often feels, are not for him. I have been most interested in the way some young men from the armed forces hate hymns and regard what I think are beautiful prayers as unreal. Ten verses from Isaiah and ten more from Revelation also seem quite unintelligible. Yet many worshipers love these things, enter into them sincerely, have all their lives been brought up on such a diet, and would miss it if it were withdrawn.

Another group, I find, especially of very busy people, loves the worshipful part of a service, but has no use for the sermon. Men say they can read sermons at home, or hear better ones on the radio. They love good music and the sense of corporate worship in a brief service of half an hour.

Many want to ask questions. Frankly I have been surprised at the sensible nature of the questions sent in. They are almost all either theological, or, less frequently, questions about the relation between Christianity and the social order, or personal questions—"What should a person do if . . . ?"—obviously the questioner's own problem wrapped up to look like someone else's.

Many young people want fellowship. I was greatly criticized for offering coffee and cakes in the schoolroom after our so-called experimental services. People wrote literally from all over the world because reports—often garbled and highly colored—appeared in the press. But I am quite unrepentant, though I was charged with bribing people with coffee to come to church. Yet Jesus spoke of the value and importance of the "cup of cold water" given to the little ones, and the Western modern equivalent is a cup of tea or coffee.

At the social hour which followed, young people met one another. They met my workers and me. They were told about our every-night-of-the-week organizations and challenged to admit they were lonely in London after a month with us! I have evidence that some young folk who found Christian fellowship with us would have been driven by sheer loneliness to find fellowship in much less desirable ways.

To suit all the types I have described above, we therefore arranged the following occasional evening services:

6:30–6:55. Worship. Very good and carefully chosen music, with anthem, brief readings from the Bible and the other great literature of the world, a number of short prayers with sung "Amen," the Lord's Prayer intoned, and a period for silent adoration.

Interval, with organ music during which people could enter or leave the church.

7:00–7:25. Sermon on some topic which illustrated the relevance of Jesus' message and ministry, his death and resurrection, to the life of men and women today.

Interval as above.

7:30–8:00. Questions written down on slips of paper are handed up to the pulpit by a steward and answered on the spot. It is unwise to allow people to *ask* questions. They usually cannot be heard all over the church, and there is much craning of necks to see who is speaking. Further, one cannot exclude the crank and fanatic. One can tear up the paper if a silly question is written down, and not have time wasted by futile discussions about cranky subjects.

Interval for adjournment to schoolroom or lecture hall.

8:15–9:15. Social intercourse with refreshments, ending with family prayers at the end.

The questions handed in intrigued me most. I tried to answer most of them, but many demanded far more care than I could bestow under the circumstances described above. It seemed to me that they were honestly asked. I got the impression that in many cases the seeker had gone to the Bible to get his answer and been puzzled by it. "Thy word is a lamp unto my feet, and a light unto my path," says the psalmist. But, for one reason or another, though the light of truth shines forth from the Bible as from no other source, the meaning is often far from clear. The lamp flickers and seems to give an uncertain light.

So I took a score of the questions sent in and answered them from the pulpit at greater length and with greater detail than was previously possible. These discourses, with some others asked earlier and preached in a series of sermons called "What Did Jesus Really Mean?" are the basis for this book. They were not given in close series, and the ideas in some are repeated in others. They nearly all refer to puzzling passages in the New Testament and to words which Jesus is reported to have used. I send them out in the hope that they may make some small contribution to our understanding of him who spake as never man spake, and that his shining truth may illumine the dark path we have to tread.

Many questions commonly asked are omitted because I have dealt with them in other books. For instance, one of the questions sent up every time we invited them at the City Temple was, "Why do we pray 'Lead us not into temptation'? Surely God would not in any case do that." This I tried to answer in *Jesus and Ourselves*. The questions relative to pacifism I tried to answer in *Thinking Aloud in Wartime*, and the problem of the coin in the fish's mouth I commented on in *It Happened in Palestine*, "Take no thought for the morrow" in *Why Do Men Suffer?* and the feeding of the five thousand in *A Shepherd Remembers*. I should weary the reader by further citation.

Warmest thanks are due to my secretary, Miss Winifred Haddon, for unstinted help in preparing this book for the press.

LESLIE D. WEATHERHEAD

The City Temple
c/o Marylebone Presbyterian Church
George Street, Marble Arch
London, W.1.

Contents

I

Did Jesus Distinguish Between Sacred and Secular?

WHEREVER I GO, I AM VERY CONCERNED TO FIND THAT THE COMMONest criticism of modern religion is that it seems irrelevant to life. The criticisms of cranks can be overlooked. The criticisms which are smoke screens concealing from themselves the real motives of those who want an excuse for slackness can be disregarded. But the criticisms of thoughtful men and women must be considered. Many such people really do love God and their neighbors, and they believe in religion, but the services of the churches leave them cold, and many of the week-night activities seem little removed from those of a club. Indeed, many say that they find better fellowship in a club, for there is less gossip, less tittle-tattle, less meanness, less bitterness, and fewer hurt feelings over trifles.

The commonest criticism that I hear of sermons is that they do not deal with the problems ordinary men and women are facing, that they talk a language remote from everyday living, that much of the sermon time is given to biblical and theological problems which do not seem to bear upon life at all, and that the language used is often a preacher's jargon which means little to the layman. In a word, that religion is not apparently related to life, and that is a damning indictment. If ever religion comes to be thought of as something remote from everyday life, we shall never be able to make the new world about which we have spoken much, thought a little, and prayed occasionally.

Let me start here. I don't think we can remind ourselves too often that the whole of creation is a *uni*-verse. It is not a multi-verse. From the smallest atom to the farthest star one will, one mind, one spirit holds everything together. Law, which we call the law of nature, is the law of God, and that law sweeps majestically through the whole universe.

The scientist must, again and again, be thrilled to feel this unity of law. Sodium burns with a yellow flame in the laboratory and with a yellow flame in the sun. The laws of reflected light are the same whether a boy reflects them with a mirror on a sunny afternoon or whether the moon reflects them on a cold winter night. God reigns throughout all creation, and his sovereign will directs it.

Then realize that on this little planet, this little wayside world on which our lot has been cast, the reign of law is dominant throughout. True, man has been given free will and in many ways—not all—can oppose the will of God. But through every phase of man's activity—physical, mental, spiritual—sweep the majestic laws which are the expression of God's mind and will and purposes. You cannot *break* law. If you resist it, you can be broken by it. If you are ignorant of it, or through folly or sin run counter to it, you can suffer terribly. It is a false use of language to say that you can *break* the law of God. Nothing breaks it. It breaks us. For if man resists it, runs up against it, behaves as though it were not there, he always suffers. If he opposes physical laws, he suffers physically and usually quite quickly. If he opposes mental laws, suffering may be delayed, but it is certain. If he opposes spiritual laws, consequences may be delayed until man reaches another phase of life—the life that goes on when the material body has returned to the dust of the universe—but that life in the unseen is still in the universe. Man can never escape from the universe, and because God is the Person whose will and mind make it a *uni*-verse, man is never outside those majestic energies, and should he set himself against them, he can never ultimately win. He cannot even defy them with impunity.

Again, we can never remind ourselves too often that the universe exists for God. In a sense it does not exist for man. It was created for spiritual ends, *and none of its energies can be twisted finally to prosper any purposes but God's.*

This is so important that I want to emphasize it even further. It is *God's* universe. It is *his* law. It is *his* mind. It is *his* will. Throughout every part of it, the unseen as well as the seen, the processes of thought as well as the arrangement of molecules, run *his* purposes. And if man tries to wrest from them some miserable little advantage for himself, if he tries to tap the resources of the universe to make hell for other people, if he sits down in a corner with only selfish aims in mind and thinks that the universe will contribute to *his* wealth or *his* selfish aims or *his* superiority over others, he will only find himself deluded, and the name of that delusion is hell. To put an illustration into a sentence or two, the idea of the brotherhood of man is not just a pious, religious, impractical ideal. It is a law of the universe, and if man acts in an unbrotherly way, he will be broken; that is all. World co-operation in a brotherly spirit under the fatherhood of God is not just a cranky idea which certain religious fanatics preach and believe. It is part of that end to which the whole creation moves, and to move away from it, however plausibly, to act selfishly, however satisfyingly for the moment, is to move nearer to disaster. As Gamaliel hinted so long ago, you cannot fight against God and win.[1]

If the universe exists only for God, the only *good* we can get out of it is that which comes to us when we are in harmony with the mind and will and purposes of God, no longer seeking to fight them or resist them or twist them to bring apparent gain for ourselves. The only thing that is *good* in the universe is that good for which the universe was created, namely, spiritual good.

If all this is true, then obviously life should be conterminous with religion, and a truly religious attitude and experience would integrate life. That integration man sorely needs, for without it he cannot make sense of life. Religion will never do its work in the world if it is so misunderstood as to be regarded as an interest which some people take up and some people do not, like golf or music or collecting stamps. Religion is relevant to every man's whole being. Indeed, it is his life that is irrelevant and largely meaningless without religion. The people who admit that they live for business or pleasure or their home, and yet who leave out God, are surprised that they are so continually at sixes and sevens within themselves, so often unhappy and bewildered, but they are trying to make life work out to *their* ends. On the physical plane they often keep the rules and often seem physically healthy, but on the spiritual plane they are doing something as foolish, and finally as catastrophic, as the neglect of the simple rules of health would be on the physical plane. Let me repeat it. This is a *uni*-verse. You cannot merely keep the rules on the physical and mental planes and not bother about the spiritual. The whole universe exists for spiritual ends. As D. [illegible]

[1]Read Acts 5, especially vs. 39.

Davies once said, in a pregnant sentence which I commend to you, "Outside God *there is only death*."

I find at the moment among people a great unrest, a great bewilderment, a great sense of futility, a tendency to keep the mind distracted by trifles and never to sit down to think—as if man could keep a precarious hold on sanity and escape the dread darkness of meaninglessness by never giving the mind time to contemplate life.

There are many causes of this unhappy state of things. During the war we were working toward an end. It was victory. That purposefulness co-ordinated life. In a sense it integrated life. We were shoulder to shoulder in a great cause, and until the cause was carried through, we did not stay to contemplate further issues. Furthermore, there was a sense of brotherhood about. We did not like the people in our street very much perhaps, but we co-operated with them in fire watching. We did not like the other folks in the shelter, but a common terror made us one. We were of all shades of political opinion, but we supported a national government. But now what has happened? Victory has come—I almost added "and gone"! I say no political word at the moment, but I see on the horizon no sign of the city of dreams coming any nearer. I look round the world in vain to find a country that is contented and happy, let alone blessed. It is hardly exaggerating to say that every section of every community is in a state of revolt, and the strikes and discord and dissatisfaction in our own country are reflected in almost every country in the world, and are but the macrocosm of the state of our own minds.

But I am quite sure there is another cause—largely overlooked—for the present state of things. It is man's refusal to be religious. It is man's damned humanism, and I am using that word rightly. It *is* damned. It has been condemned for centuries. It has been tried again and again and been found to fail. Man will not believe that he is anything more than a higher animal with a certain culture which has come to him from others—many of them Christian—through the centuries. Yet all the time there is a God within him crying out that the universe exists for spiritual purposes, and that there is an integrating goal ahead, far greater than any military victory in the world: man's chief end is to glorify God and enjoy *him*. But man refuses all this. Whether it is the fault of the churches or his own slackness, we will not consider now, but he will have nothing to do with religion and finds himself in a conflict which is all the more threatening because it is largely unconscious. Man does not realize that in refusing to align himself with the mighty spiritual purposes for which the universe was created he is doing despite to his own true self, going against his highest nature, doing to his soul what he would do to his body if he neglected all the simple rules of health. The city of personal human nature is divided against itself and cannot stand. So man will sit down and plan and scheme, take that government out and put this government in, hold this conference in Paris and that in New York, give his men of science free rein to discover things like atomic energy, but he will not realize that he is a spiritual person in the hands of a supreme spiritual Being, that he is in existence at all only in order that he may achieve a spiritual goal. He is not an animal functioning on a planet, not even a higher animal functioning on a civilized planet, but an immortal spirit functioning in the eternal universe of God, and he always will be bewildered, defeated, distressed, and at war within and without until he brings himself into harmony with God.

I want you to see that we cannot live outside *God's* universe except by artificiality, and to attempt to do so is as senseless as it is harmful. I want to plead with you for what, for many, will be a new way of regarding religion. Truly religious people should not be those who live in a little world of their own where they say their prayers, go to services, enjoy the "consolations of religion," have little devotional experiences, and believe that God is interested only in what they call "religious work." Do take seriously the view that real religion is conterminous with the whole of life, not something behind an iron curtain from which we emerge to do the work of "the world." What I am about to say is liable to misunderstanding, but I must risk that. All life for the *really* religious man is life in God's world. It is fatal to have one foot in God's world and the other in a different kind of world altogether. The division exists only in a mind that is thinking falsely, for the world of the worldly is a fantasy. It isn't real at all. If I had my way, I would cut out from our vocabulary adjectives like "worldly" and nouns like "worldliness." I know that there is immense value in warning young people about phases of life that cannot contribute to their spiritual well-being, and I know that the saints call that worldliness, but what I am trying to say is that the religious man integrates all the activities of life and does not see two worlds but *one*, and that one shot through and through with the beauty and purposes of God.

Now even the church has offended against this conception, and it has done so in several ways.

1. It has divided activities into the sacred and the secular. I am said to be engaged in a sacred task and my shoemaker in a secular task. But the religious man should not hold that distinction as valid. The religious shoemaker is as much a servant of God as the man who hands you the sacrament. He is, in fact, in God's world doing God's work for God's people for God's sake. Indeed, he is co-operating with God in guarding the health of his people in wet weather. He is helping God answer the prayers of his people for health. Because he is a *religious* shoemaker, he cannot put cardboard instead of leather into shoes. Making a good pair of shoes thoroughly is a divine service because it is a contribution to the welfare of men, and service to men is the only way of *serving* God. When we get more sense, we shall ordain shoemakers, and charwomen who really come at eight in the morning, and maids who do not give notice after their first rebuff from the mistress. We shall ordain bus drivers and railway men and carpenters and plumbers and so on. It was when Jesus had been a carpenter for twenty years and had never preached a single sermon, that the Voice said, "This is my beloved Son, in whom I am well pleased."

If once we could get this idea really operating, we could "Christianize industry," as the phrase goes, and religion could unify all industry if industry could be seen to be an expression of the work of God in the world. Let the church stop talking about sacred and secular, and send into society her sons and daughters who will live always in God's world whether they make soap or make sermons, whether they light a fire of coals in the grate or a fire of faith in the heart of another.

God is not the copyright of religion, and God's ways are not to be expressed only in theological jargon, nor God's activities carried out in what is called religious work. As Browning says, "All service ranks the same with God." We shall never unify the world until we see it all to be God's world and until a man interprets his religion in terms of his own job and stops thinking that God is interested in him only if he takes a Sunday-school class, or shows people into their pews, or preaches sermons, or helps to run a church.

2. The church has sinned in this regard also in implying that there is

something ungodly in appreciating the joys of the senses. In olden days the saints talked much about "withdrawing from the world," but their Master did not withdraw from the world. He did not climb up a mountain and live in a cave as an ascetic, to be consulted as an oracle by men who made a pilgrimage to a lonely, withdrawn figure. He climbed up the mountain for prayer—and I would not speak one word which would seem to disparage the value and necessity of set times of prayer—but then he came down into the world and enjoyed himself so much that his happiness became a scandal. He was called "the friend of publicans and sinners." "This man receiveth sinners, *and eateth with them.*" "A gluttonous man, and a winebibber," they said, because, frankly, he loved to go to parties, *and all the time he was living in God's world.* I expect he was the life and soul of the party. I should like a manuscript to be discovered which said that he told funnier stories than anybody and had the table in a roar of happy mirth. Indeed, through all his parables the grace of a lovely humor lightens the lessons he tried to teach. It is incongruous to hear the fun taken out of his stories. It is sometimes really funny to hear some solemn, ponderous parson trying to pretend that there is no humor in Christ's words, and reading the story of the man who choked at a fly and swallowed a camel, or of the man who put his lamp under the bed instead of on the lampstand, or of the man who couldn't come to a feast because he had married a wife, and so on—with a score of other illustrations one could give—as if the words "Here beginneth the first lesson" must necessarily precede some solemn exhortation from which all humor must be rigorously excluded.

Jesus did not *withdraw* from the world, for *there is nowhere else to go.* It is *all* God's world. The saints who started the theater—and you will remember that the first plays were in churches and only the ordained were allowed to play them—were far more in harmony with Christ's mind than the Victorians who thought it wicked to go to the theater. Jesus said that when the prodigal came home there was a tremendous feast and plenty of dancing. Yet many of our young people have a suspicion that religion frowns upon them if they stay out late at a dance. The saints in medieval times got up at a dreadful hour in the morning to say their prayers and tried not to enjoy their meals too openly because of this twisted conception that it is wrong to enjoy the delights of the senses which God has provided for our enjoyment. And, of course, as for sex—in many narrow minds and hearts that is still taboo. Everything regarding it is supposed to be unclean. It is wicked to think about it, let alone talk about it, and I am still waiting for a great saint to say openly that he has enjoyed it. I myself have suffered in a dozen ways by trying to kill the stupid taboo on sex, trying to bring it out into the open, and trying to show it to be a healthy, lovely expression of God's will for us, as clean as the wind and as beautiful as flowers.

The really religious man, I say, knows only one world, and it is God's world. Every expression of it that is not inherently evil is baptized into God's spirit, and until we can integrate life like that, the church will never do its work in the world. It will stand outside and regard suspiciously whole areas of man's happiest and busiest activities, as though they were entirely outside the divine interest and had nothing to do with the divine plan. Churchmen *will* cling to that stupid attitude that God would the more smile upon their life the more they withdrew from the world he created to be their home, and the place where they were destined to meet him.

So the church says to the layman, "Give up some of your time to God." But it is all God's. There must be a time for praying, of course, because prayer is as essential to the life of the soul as eating to the life of the body. But it is all God's time, and when a religious man is doing his business honestly, he is giving his time to God. "Do all your work to God's glory," people say, as though an alien, hostile thing were being dedicated. But when man is doing his work honestly, thoroughly, and happily, he is already doing it to the glory of God and giving the time he takes to God. All true values in life are God's, not just those which we happen to label religious.

I now want to say something which is even more likely to cause misunderstanding, but I think it is important. This attitude of living always in God's world will become most healthy when it is least conscious. Now let me try to get this right. We have spoken so often of the importance of daily prayer that I will say no more about that. What is equally true is that if man can consciously turn to God half a dozen times during the day, he is much more likely to keep his life sweet and clean. But let him never suppose that he must try to think consciously of God through all the hours of a working day, any more than a child is conscious of his relationship with his father all through the hours of a day. If the child, or, shall we say, the young adolescent, is asked about it, he will explain just what his father means to him (I am imagining an ideal relationship), but he will not, if studying, consciously think during every university lecture or hour in the classroom, "My father is paying my fees, and I must be worthy of him." The relationship is *there*. Unconsciously it is wielding a great influence, but it is the more healthy the less it is conscious. I was startled to hear Dr. Temple say once that a religious man should forget God for most of the day, but it was the truth that startled me. A man may be engaged in his business in order to make a lovely home for his wife and give all the benefits he honestly can to his children, but he must not start thinking about his wife in the midst of solving a business problem. Is it irreverent to suppose that sometimes the grandest thing Jesus could do for the Kingdom of God was to forget God in order that he might concentrate entirely on making a yoke smooth in a carpenter's shop? Canon Barry tells of a preacher who went to a boys' boarding school and told the boys that they should continually think of God, and added, "Take God with you onto the athletic field." Frankly, I think that is nonsense. In a footnote Canon Barry, now Bishop of Southwell, tells of a bishop watching a game, who, when a goal was scored, was heard to utter, "That shot was richly blessed!" Barry adds that he thinks that was an ecclesiastical idiom for the more familiar "That was a damned good shot!"

Some people with the wrong idea of religion would be more truly religious if they prayed less and learned how to cook. Some people would be more truly religious if they turned off the radio religious service and paid the milkman's bill, or treated the maid as a fellow Christian, or refrained from upsetting the peace of the home by a vile temper, a nagging tongue, or a hectic atmosphere that makes the whole household unhappy. Some men would be more religious if they gave up office in the church and concentrated on the welfare of the people in the office they work in every day. And when a friend of mine says that he plays golf to the glory of God, I wish he would forget God and keep his eye on the ball. Religion has become a sort of self-conscious thing, linked up with strained attitudes and pious language. It is more and more becoming in the minds of men a thing not done. Two of my friends at a weekend house party announced they were going to church and were met with hoots of mirth, and religiosity is partly to blame. The church has said so often that life in the world is something apart from religion that now men have come to think that religion is something apart from life in the world.

Religion is life! Religion is everything. Nothing matters but religion. The universe is God's universe. Everything he created in it proclaims his glory. It exists for him, and our religion should be expressing itself through everything we do. We do not normally think about the value of food all day. We eat our breakfast and forget about food, though all the morning that food sustains us. The more unconscious digestive energies can be, the better! Let us guard our times of prayer, certainly, but let us draw upon those religious energies all day without feeling that religion must always be conscious, and let every energy of our being be an expression of the power we have drawn from God.

Let us look once more at Jesus. He always seemed so at home in his Father's world, and he lived in it all the time. He was not always talking about God or thinking about God. Sometimes he played with little children and mended their toys and went out to dinner. Sometimes he found that the highest expression of religion was to make a doorframe that fitted. When he went into the mountains to pray, he did not go from one world into another, and he never talked about worldliness. His religion was not a side show or a hobby or an interest. As my beloved teacher, William R. Maltby, once said, "His life was one whole. His mind, like his robe, was without seam, woven from the top throughout."

Can we follow Jesus there? Do not let us be religious on Sundays and give any poet reason to write the stinging couplet:

> Their worship's over, God returns to heaven
> And stays there till next Sunday at eleven.

Do not let us talk or think or act as though religious talk and religious exercises were the whole of religion. Let the sleeping love of God breathe a fragrance through every part of our lives, and if the word "fragrance" seems sentimental, let us substitute "honesty" or "industry," or the words which express that which we lack. Some religious people would do well to remember that religion includes filling out correctly their income-tax form and giving their employer an hour's devoted service of their very best quality for every hour for which he pays. And do not let us think we go out of God's world when we enjoy ourselves; and do not let us think of God as an amiable, absentee Ruler, remote from human life, but as the immanent, creative, loving, personal Force that has made the universe one and can bring harmony into our distracted lives.

So our lives can be caught up and woven into the eternal purposes of a loving God. So our religion can make sense of life, and bring us a joy and a peace that we never knew before.

II

Did Jesus Repudiate the Old Testament?

It hath been said . . . , but I say . . . —Matt. 5:43-44

IT IS NO DISPARAGEMENT OF THE OLD TESTAMENT TO STATE QUITE definitely that the revelation of the nature of God which we find in it is gradual. Some people imagine that although science is continually brought up to date and its older views discarded, religion, because its approach to truth is different, is content to be static. Science finds its way by experiment and discovery; religion finds its way by experience and revelation. But in a sense these are two aspects of the same thing. Nothing could be discovered unless God revealed it, and nothing is revealed until men discover it. The scientist of today repudiates the scientific assertions which passed as truth a hundred years ago. Science corrects its former judgments by new discoveries; religion corrects its former judgments by new insights, and the religious man must be allowed the same freedom to repudiate the false ideas of earlier days.

Many who will admit so much believe that Jesus Christ is the last word in man's discovery of God, and that therefore all progress in our religious thinking ends in the manifestation of him who was God's Son, who was the fullest expression of God that any human life could carry. But even so, inasmuch as we are still exploring the character and teaching of Jesus and still finding new implications and relevances in what he said and was, progress goes on and will go on until, if ever, all that he said and was and is, is exhausted by human understanding.

Some of the parts of the Old Testament were written hundreds of years before Christ, and it is incredible that there should have been no progress in men's thought about God from those early times until the present day. While we may find in the Old Testament words expressing such spiritual insight that they may still be used to clothe our own ideas and aspirations, that true fact ought not to blind us to another fact that *some* verbal pictures of God in the Old Testament are inadequate, that *some* words which describe God cannot possibly be true, that *some* teaching concerning the ways of God to men is utterly misleading. And just as a scientist would find himself in unutterable confusion if he sought to meet the demands of today with the scientific knowledge of, say, the first century, so a modern Christian who really loves truth must be ready at truth's behest to relinquish those ideas about God which belong to a time when men had not thought their way through the problems they tackled, and had not received the light which Jesus threw upon the nature and methods of God.

Write down, if you will, on the back of an envelope, but certainly on the tablet of your memory, this basic principle: *Every idea about God is wrong if, when truly understood, it conflicts essentially with that picture of God which Jesus Christ gave the world in his words and in his life.* However dear to you the words of the Old Testament may be, however you may have hugged them to your heart in some moment of need, however they reflect what you would like to believe is true, part from them, discard them, throw them away, if, in the light of Jesus or when confronted by the stern reality of truth—and these two are the same—they are obviously false. Only by so doing can you obey what Jesus called the greatest commandment and love God with all your mind; only by so doing can you find an anchorage for the soul in times of stress, which is sure and reliable; only so can you find a refuge which will not fall in upon you when you need it most. So many people in their latter years are in despair because what they thought was truth—often culled from the Old Testament—has let them down, and they have had, in the evening of their lives, either to relinquish their faith altogether—and what a pathetic spectacle that can be—or with trembling hands to try to build up for themselves a fabric of faith that can stand up to the grim realities among which we now live. I think that is what David Gascoyne meant by these words:

> Far from Thy face I nothing understand,
> But kiss the Hand that hath consigned
> Me to these latter years, where I must learn
> The revelation of despair, and find

Among the debris of all certainties
The hardest stone on which to found
Altar and shelter for Eternity.[1]

We can see in a very few sentences what an immense development there is in man's thought about God as we pass from the atmosphere of the Old Testament to that of the New. At the beginning of the Old, God is thought of so anthropomorphically, so much in the form of a man, that he walks in the garden in the cool of the day,[2] shows to Moses his back,[3] is so localized that he lives on Mount Sinai and can be thought of as being with his chosen people only when they carry with them a box called the ark, in which he is supposed to dwell. Compare with that picture of God this: "God is spirit: and they that worship him must worship in spirit and truth." [4] In early Old Testament times God was a tribal God. He loved his chosen people, but hated his enemies. Think of the difference in atmosphere when you read "God so loved the *world*." [5] In the Old Testament, God was regarded with dread, and the people said to Moses, "Let not God speak with us, lest we die." [6] But Jesus said, "When ye pray, say, Our Father." [7] As you realize this immense development of thought, try to realize that *it is still going on*. Men now have the picture of God which Jesus gave and which Jesus was, but, more and more, those who have spiritual insight, and who spend time in prayer, find a growing understanding of the meaning and relevance of the amazing things that Jesus revealed about God.

The Old Testament remains a wonderful collection of spiritually valuable books reflecting a level of religion incomparably superior to that of the tribes with which the Hebrew people were in conflict. The religion of the Old Testament, with its grand emphasis on ethical morality and its amazing insistence on one God, lifts itself up like a pure lotus lily rising from some stagnant and filthy pool. But I hope that what I have said already has established my first point, that it is no disparagement of the Old Testament to realize that, since those days, men's

[1] Used by permission Poetry London, publishers.
[2] Gen. 3:8.
[3] Exod. 33:23.
[4] John 4:24 Revised Version margin.
[5] John 3:16.
[6] Exod. 20:19.
[7] Luke 11:2.

thoughts have moved on, and we only subject our minds to unnecessary torture by trying to retain—as if they were adequate for these days, or as if piety demanded their retention—those pictures of God and those thoughts about God's ways with men which, in the name of truth, we are called upon to discard.

Let us now apply that thought of progress in religious thinking to some of the problems that many people are trying to face in the light of the Old Testament, when they should be trying to face them in the light of the New.

1. Let us first consider the problem of physical safety. A great many people believe that if they trust God, say their prayers, and live a good life, God will keep them, and the loved ones for whom they pray, safe from all physical harm. A dear friend of mine who is a most devout Christian confided to me that if his boy did not come back from Norway, he would lose his faith. Alas! the boy's body lies at the bottom of a Norwegian fiord. In Old Testament days men were taught that they could rely on a kind of bargain with God: If a man trusts in God, it is up to God to take care of him. As Ps. 91:7 says, "A thousand shall fall at thy side, and ten thousand at thy right hand; but it shall not come nigh thee." Again and again we could pick up sentences out of the psalms that speak of God as a shelter, as a defense, as a strong tower; and if we spiritualize them, we may still use these words today, but those who wrote them down meant by them that God would provide physical security. But come into the light of the New Testament. Jesus did not talk like that.[8] Jesus, in other words, never promised safety to his men. Tradition says that every one of them was martyred. He never said, "If you follow me, you will be taken care of." He said the opposite, "If you follow me, you will get into trouble." They were not to expect a magical protection from those physical dangers which assail everybody. On the contrary, they were to expect not only what other men have to face, but hostility and persecution, which would be their lot just because they were his. Indeed, men who killed them would think that they did God service.[9]

In the following passage you find the same attitude of the Master.

[8] The last verses of Mark's Gospel (vs. 18 onward) are acknowledged by all scholars to have been added by another hand after the end of the Gospel as Mark wrote it had been lost. It probably got worn away with constant use, as the parchment or papyrus on which it was written was passed round the early churches.

[9] Matt. 10:16-28; John 15:20; 16:2.

"Suppose ye," he says, "that these Galilaeans [who were put to death] were sinners above all the Galilaeans . . .? I tell you, Nay. . . . Or those eighteen, upon whom the tower in Siloam fell, and slew them, that they were sinners above all men that dwelt in Jerusalem? I tell you, Nay." [10] There is no magical insurance against physical peril for Christ's followers. Religion would be unspeakably degraded if it were so, and to be religious would be a wonderful insurance policy to take out, for the dividend would be the guarantee of personal safety, however foolish or fatuous one might be, or whatever peril one encountered. The flower of physical courage would be cut through at the root, for if one is guaranteed safety, one has no need to be courageous.

A friend of mine put his perplexity thus to me: "I don't think much of a God who cannot take care of my boy when I pray for him every night." But we must be realistic in all this. It is not a question of what God cannot do. No human being knows enough to answer that question. It is a matter of what God *must not* do, and clearly he *must not* make religion an insurance. He *must not* have favorites. You would even despise a schoolmaster who always saw to it that your boy never suffered with the others. God *must not* interfere, in answer to prayer, in order to do for his children what they must learn to do by themselves. He *must not* allow the answer to an individual prayer to militate against the final well-being of the whole human family, or encourage men to believe falsely and hopelessly.

Now don't misunderstand me to say you are not to pray for your loved ones. Of course you must pray for them, and if you want to do so, pray for their safety. But if God must not answer that particular prayer, don't lose your faith. Let me underline this: *If God can answer your prayer for your physical safety, or that of your loved ones, without being less than God, he will do so.* But remember that man's spirit is the real man, not his body, and that is always safe from physical accident and injury. The body of Jesus himself was murdered. It was his spirit he committed to God.

Come, then, from the atmosphere of the Old Testament, where you may find the argument "If I trust in God, he will keep me safe," into the atmosphere of the New Testament, where God's own Son is not safe, but where the calamity that happened to him was woven at last

[10] Luke 13:2-5.

into the fabric of a divine purpose, too big and too splendid and too glorious for the compass of our little minds. After all, which sounds the deeper note in religion, "You will be safe if you trust," or "God is counting on you to trust him, whatever happens, for nothing can finally defeat him. Nothing can happen to you that cannot be woven into his plans"?

2. Turn from that to the allied subject of suffering, and look at that in the light of this truth about the development of thought. Every minister knows those sad moments when he visits someone who is suffering and who is tormented with the thought "What have I done to deserve this?" I was asked recently to go to see a man suffering from cancer. He was almost too ill to speak, and I could tell that his mind was in torture because he whispered, in a voice of infinite pathos, "Is it because I have sinned that I am suffering like this?"

Do try to get this straight. In the Old Testament people who suffered did look back and sought to find in past sins the cause of present suffering. *But in the New Testament people look forward.* They believe that though their suffering is not the will of God, but has befallen them as part of the burden of the whole world's ignorance and folly and sin, it can be used of God to build up something splendid and glorious in the future. Let me repeat that, because it is of such immense importance. In the Old Testament people look back, and they see present suffering as punishment for past sin. In the New Testament people look forward, certain that the clue to the spiritual meaning of present suffering lies, not in the past, but in the future. Job's enemies, as I call them—he called them his friends—said, "You must have done something terrible. God would not allow the righteous to suffer. Now, face it! What have you been doing?" [11] But listen to Paul in the New Testament, for remember that, though Paul had healed other people, he suffered lifelong disability himself. "I besought the Lord thrice," he says, "that it might depart from me. And he said unto me, My grace is sufficient for thee: for my strength is made perfect in weakness. Most gladly therefore will I rather glory in my infirmities, that the power of Christ may rest upon me." [12] Notice the looking forward—"that the power of Christ *may rest* upon me." As though the great apostle is saying, "I am not going to look back and try to imagine why I suffer like this. Apparently I have to bear it. I

[11] See Job 4:7.
[12] II Cor. 12:8-9.

shall not get out of it because I am Christ's man. For a reason that is not clear to me God's intentional will, namely perfect health, cannot yet be done, but Christ and I together are going to build something grand out of all this." Listen again to a passage that points to the future for the clue to present suffering: "No chastening for the present seemeth to be joyous, but grievous: nevertheless afterward it yieldeth the peaceable fruit of righteousness." [13] Or again, "Our light affliction, *which is but for a moment,* worketh for us a far more exceeding and eternal weight of glory."[14]

There are, of course, some forms of suffering concerning which we can legitimately look back and say, "This is caused by that." If you run your head into a stone pillar, then later you may be lying down with a headache and saying, "Why have I to suffer thus?" The answer there is obvious. But even there pain is the consequence, not of sin, but of folly, and I feel I cannot sufficiently emphasize two important sentences:

a) The *consequence* of sin—and the consequence of ignorance and folly—may be physical suffering, but the *punishment* of sin is in the soul. It is moral deterioration and separation from God.

b) All sin brings suffering, but all suffering is not due to sin.

I hope you can perceive the important logic here. Those who have studied logic are familiar with the fallacy involved. All greyhounds are dogs. But you cannot turn that round and say, therefore, all dogs are greyhounds. Similarly, all sin causes suffering; but you must not turn that round and say, therefore, all suffering is caused by sin. Suffering is often the fruit of ignorance and folly on the part of others, bound to us by the ties which bind the human family together.

If I could speak quite frankly to those who insist that suffering is punishment for sin, I would put it crudely thus. Venereal disease is often chosen as an illustration which is supposed to prove that God punishes immorality with suffering. When a person develops venereal disease, he himself presumably looks back and thinks, "This is caused by that." Yes, the *consequence* of his sin is venereal disease, but the punishment of that sin is in the soul, not in the body, for obviously venereal disease can be prevented. If discovered early, it can be cured. Do you mean, then, that God is rendered incapable of punishing the sinner if the sinner remembers to use preventives when sinning, or to seek early treatment

[13] Heb. 12:11.
[14] II Cor. 4:17.

when the so-called punishment becomes apparent? Consequence may or may not be avoided. Punishment never!

Or in regard to cancer, how can a man regard cancer as a punishment for sin, since one of these days we shall know how to prevent it and how to cure it? On that glad day when we learn how to prevent or cure cancer, shall we have balked God so that he cannot punish people any more in that way? If, as many people hold, cancer is the will of God, and used by him to punish people for sin, then when we cure cancer shall we have done the will of God, or outwitted God? Imagine a man, because he has found the cure for cancer, turning round to God, as it were, and saying, "Ah! you can't punish men now by giving them cancer, because we can cure it. We have outwitted you." I put it this way only to show how absurd it is really to regard suffering in terms of punishment. I hold most strongly that, when cancer is cured, we shall have done the will of God in the name of him who went about healing all manner of disease. The punishment of sin is in the soul; the consequences of sin may, or may not, be in the body. All sin causes suffering, but all suffering is not due to sin. And I do beseech you to come out of the atmosphere of the Old Testament, where men morbidly looked back to the past for the clue to suffering, into the atmosphere of the New, in which men—while they may, or may not, recognize causation in the past—see the *spiritual* clue in the future, and find even delight in thinking that the affliction of the present is something which, in co-operation with God, they can build up into something splendid, even though that something is at present beyond the horizon of their vision.

3. Apply the same theme to the thought of immortality, which is in so many minds at the moment. We may dismiss the Old Testament view in a few moments. Again and again men tremble at the approach of death, plead with God for long life, and regard "many days" as a sign of his blessing. Note:

With *long life* will I satisfy him, and show him my salvation. (Ps. 91:16.)

What man is he that desireth life, and loveth *many days*, that he may see good? (Ps. 34:12.)

All our days are passed away in thy wrath. (Ps. 90:9.)

So teach us to number our days, that we may apply unto our hearts wisdom. (Ps. 90:12.)

As for man, his days are as grass. (Ps. 103:15.)

Honour thy father and thy mother: *that thy days may be long* upon the land which the Lord thy God giveth thee. (Exod. 20:12.)

Take up that last sentence, one of the Ten Commandments, taught to every modern child. Yet on examination the second part of it is utter nonsense. What possible connection is there between honoring one's parents and living a long time? Methuselah certainly must have been incredibly kind to the old folks at home! One can see the thought behind it, of course. To honor one's parents is a good thing, and in the sight of the men of the Old Testament to live many days was a divine reward. But how pathetic is this longing for years and years! How erroneous to suppose that the mere gift of days is a sign of God's special love! Mere years only turn a young sinner into an old sinner, a young fool into an old fool. And what do we make of that old-fashioned thought that length of days is a proof of good character, when we remember that some of the very greatest men and women died young, and when every night during the war for our liberty, young men gave up their life in the early twenties? But, you see, in Old Testament times they did not really believe in life after death. In some tenuous sort of ghostly existence, perhaps, but not in *life*. We will not go into what existence in Sheol really meant, but it was always regarded as vague and ghostly. And so men asked God that before the dread time came, before the dark mists of death fell upon the spirit and joy passed away from existence, they might have many days of real living.

What a different atmosphere in the New Testament! Paul says that he really cannot decide what to choose: "I am in a strait betwixt two, having a desire to depart, and to be with Christ; *which is far better*." [15] And when he is giving instruction to Timothy, when the old warrior is talking to the young knight just buckling on his armor, he says, "I am now ready to be offered, and the time of my departure is at hand. I have fought a good fight, I have finished my course, I have kept the faith: *henceforth there is laid up for me a crown of righteousness*." [16] In other words, a more glorious life still.

I should be sadly misunderstood if I were supposed to mean that I should not grieve if my own loved ones passed away. I don't know what I should do without them. It is human and natural to love the hand-

[15] Phil. 1:23.
[16] II Tim. 4:6-8.

clasp, the light of the eyes, the sound of beloved voices. But though grief is inevitable, despair is unchristian. That dark horror of night that is still associated in the minds of some people with death belongs to the Old Testament. The New Testament is full, not of hope, but of certainty. I am more certain about the survival of the soul after death than about any other tenet in the whole Christian creed. For those who live in the New Testament there is no such thing as loss of life. There is only a fuller life on a new and happier plane. Death in the New Testament means putting off an old suit of clothes and putting on another; or going to sleep on a dark and stormy evening, and waking up and finding the sun shining; or going from a poky little slum to another, larger room, spacious and beautiful with a view of mountains and sea.

I think really we ought to come to feel about death as we feel about our summer holidays. Let me speak for myself. I am glad to have work to do. I like doing it. The discipline of having to do it by a certain time is good for me. I am not always thinking about holidays or chafing under the discipline of toil. But oh! what a joyous day that is when I slam down the lid of a big suitcase containing the books I have long wanted to read, containing tennis racket and flannels, and strong shoes for the mountains, field glasses to watch the birds, a camera, and all the other joyous things one associates with a holiday and hardly uses at all in the stuffy madhouse we call London. What a moment when one actually starts for the station! The telephone can ring all day, and the hall can fill with letters, but I am off to my father's old home in Scotland or the Yorkshire moors for recreation and exhilaration and life. The more we live in the New Testament the more, I think, we shall feel like that about death. When our loved ones die, we are sad and lonely, but after all they have gone for their holidays. They are out in the upland, sunny spaces. They are striding over the mountaintops. They are breathing the pure air of heaven. They are looking upon a loveliness which we poor slum dwellers have never seen.

Forgive me for saying that I have some right to feel like this. I have seen many people die. I have never seen anybody die unhappy. The last few moments, or even hours, are frequently wrapped round with sleep and unconsciousness, and the reflex action which may move the limbs at such a time must not be interpreted as felt pain, though it is sometimes called the agony of death. But when folk are conscious, I have seen eyes shining with rapture, and the whole countenance illumined with "the light that never was, on sea or land," a light you never see under any other circumstances. For those who believe, dying seems to be an experience of incredible happiness.

Don't live in the Old Testament. We don't belong to that old dispensation. Come out of its atmosphere without delay! There are, admittedly, patches of sunshine, but oh, so many shadows to frighten you. You are children of the day. Why cling to the shadows? "The dayspring from on high hath visited us, to give light to them that sit in darkness and in the shadow of death, to guide our feet into the way of peace."

III

Why Didn't Jesus Condemn an Adulteress?

And early in the morning he came again into the temple, and all the people came unto him; and he sat down, and taught them. And the scribes and Pharisees brought unto him a woman taken in adultery; and when they had set her in the midst, they say unto him, Master, this woman was taken in adultery, in the very act. Now Moses in the law commanded us, that such should be stoned: but what sayest thou? This they said, tempting him, that they might have to accuse him. But Jesus stooped down, and with his finger wrote on the ground, as though he heard them not. So when they continued asking him, he lifted up himself, and said unto them, He that is without sin among you, let him first cast a stone at her. And again he stooped down, and wrote on the ground. And they which heard it, being convicted by their own conscience, went out one by one, beginning at the eldest, even unto the last: and Jesus was left alone, and the woman standing in the midst. When Jesus had lifted up himself, and saw none but the woman, he said unto her, Woman, where are those thine accusers? hath no man condemned thee? She said, No man, Lord. And Jesus said unto her, Neither do I condemn thee: go, and sin no more. —John 8:2-11

THIS IS INDEED A PRECIOUS STORY, AND, HUMANLY SPEAKING, WE ARE lucky to have it at all, for originally it was no part of the Fourth Gospel. Scholars tell us that its language is quite different from that of the rest of the "Gospel according to St. John" and that it is more like Luke's style and should follow the end of Luke 21, as it does in some manuscripts.[1] Probably what happened was that a scribe, copying the Fourth Gospel, came to the verse "Ye judge after the flesh; I judge no man" (8:15) and in the margin of his manuscript wrote this vivid story as illustrating the verse. Then, as frequently happened, it got included by another copyist into the Gospel itself, and so we have it today.[2] It is without doubt genuine. It is so very like Christ. It is so very unlike anybody else.

[1] See Archbishop Temple, *Readings in St. John's Gospel,* I, 150; and Westcott, *Commentary on the Gospel of St. John,* p. 141.

[2] Lightfoot says we owe the story to Papias (*ca.* A.D. 60-135), who collected illustrations of the "Oracles of the Lord."

The Pharisees never appear more loathsome than they do in this story. They are not shocked by adultery. It was probably as common then as now. They seem to gloat over their victim and lick their salacious lips over the circumstances of her capture. They tell Jesus she was "taken in the very act." They are using her shame to trap the Master. They estimate no one more highly than Moses, and they have taught the people to venerate him. Mosaic law demanded the death penalty for proved adultery. And although the right of inflicting it had been taken from the Jews by Rome, if Jesus' enemies could get a statement from him which contradicted Moses, they would lower our Lord's prestige with the people and increase their own. A most plausible indictment could be brought against any religious teacher who contradicted Moses.[3]

It is this loathsome trick, more than the nature of the crime, which made Jesus hot with shame. But it is more than likely that the woman was naked or nearly so. Both the circumstance of her arrest and the plan to stone her suggest this. Women were stoned naked. And though the Pharisees were acting against the law of Rome in carrying out capital punishment, they had the law of Moses on their side and were in an ugly mood. We are told in the same chapter that they took up stones against Jesus,[4] and, however irregular and illegal the proceeding, Stephen was later stoned to death.[5]

If we imagine the woman terrified, disheveled, and her clothing torn or even stripped from her, it is not surprising to read that Jesus stooped and scribbled in the dust. He will not add his own gaze to the horror of humiliation and shame she is suffering. The eyes of men are hurting her enough already without the purest eyes in the world adding to her mental agony. Nor will this completely human Son of man promote the rising to his own consciousness of physical feelings common to all men. But they "continued asking him." He lifted himself up and said—and oh, that one could even imagine the blazing eyes and the stinging tones of his voice!—"He that is without sin among you, let him first cast a stone at her. And again he stooped down, and wrote on the ground." We need not ask what he wrote. Absurd suggestions have been made. A so-called religious film I saw pictured him writing the brave words of Daniel to

[3] See John 8:5-6.
[4] John 8:59.
[5] Acts 7:59.

King Belshazzar, "*Mene, mene, tekel upharsin.* . . . Thou art weighed in the balances, and art found wanting."[6] Even James Neill reports an incident he saw in Palestine, where a youth for a joke pushed another in the back and then, assuming "innocence and unconcern, commenced scribbling with his finger on the ground." Neill, comparing this incident with the one we are studying, adds, "Our Saviour, indignant at the hardened hypocrisy of the accusers, desired to give them an impressive rebuke by treating them with silent contempt, and, by studied and well-understood manner, affecting to be entirely indifferent to their insincere charge."[7] This seems quite wrong to me. So far from being indifferent, I feel Jesus was burning with a white flame of anger and that the simple explanation of his stooping and fingering the dust is that he did so to save embarrassing the woman, and to cover his own shame at the trick played upon him at the expense of a woman's feelings.

But that brief raising of himself showed them "a glimpse perhaps of the glowing blush upon his face, and they awoke suddenly with astonishment to a new sense of their condition and their conduct. The older men naturally felt it first and slunk away; the younger followed their example. The crowd dissolved and left Christ alone with the woman."[8] "Woman," he said, using the most respectful word by which to address any woman—the same word that he used to his own mother when he hung upon the cross—"Where are those thine accusers? hath no man condemned thee?" She said, "No man, Lord." And Jesus said unto her, "Neither do I condemn thee: go, and sin no more." Who can doubt but that the spiritual energy discharged from the personality of Jesus —an energy strong enough to drive away a crowd of Pharisees bent on stoning a woman and trapping a teacher, so that they slunk away like whipped curs—did not surge into that woman's soul and become, in terms of her re-energized will, a power that purged away adulterous desire and created a purity more passionate than the feelings it expelled?

What is the message of this precious story for us?

1. Note in the first place Christ's assessment of sin. Note the difference between his language to this woman and his language to the Pharisees or to those who make children to stumble. Listen! "Neither do I condemn thee: go, and sin no more." Now listen to this! "Ye serpents,

[6] Dan. 5:25, 27.
[7] *Palestine Explored,* p. 64.
[8] John R. Seeley, *Ecce Homo,* ch. 9.

ye generation of vipers, how can ye escape the damnation of hell?" [9] And this: "Whoso shall offend one of these little ones which believe in me, it were better for him that a millstone were hanged about his neck, and that he were drowned in the depth of the sea." [10] Such a man, in Jesus' view, is possessed by a devil, and in the popular thought of the day a devil could be dispensed with only by being drowned in deep water.[11]

Don't mistake the argument! Christ is not making light of adultery. He must have taken at least as grave a view of it as we do, though his judgment would not be distorted by our myopic attitude to sex, born of a mixture of personal frustration, ancient taboo, and the morbid preoccupation with sex which is one of the diseases of our age.

No, the argument runs that if, in his assessment, sins of hypocrisy, sins of pride, sins of cruelty, especially to children, are worse than adultery, they must rank thus with us, not making us think lightly of adultery, but making us count as even worse the things we scarcely call sin at all. This is not so with most of us. Sex sins, like adultery, label a man for life. (Some branches of the Christian Church will not even marry a divorced person, even if he or she be the "innocent party.") Pride, bad temper, refusing to make up a quarrel, spreading lies, indulging in malicious gossip, mental cruelty, and social injustice are thought lightly of. Yet sex sins, like adultery, are so often born of love. Call it misplaced love if you like. But behind the sin of a woman such as the one of whom we have been thinking is often a hunger and search for love, only to be met, not by the real thing, but by its spurious substitute, lust. Seeking to be loved for her own sake, she is loved for only her bodily charms. Yet it is the hunger to be loved that often makes such a woman fall the first time. As Jesus said of another woman who was a sinner, "She loved much." [12] Such a sin cannot be as bad as those we commit which are born of hate, even though its consequences in other lives may be worse. Christ's assessment of course is right, and it ought

[9] Matt. 23:33.

[10] Matt. 18:6.

[11] The bedeviled swine ran down a steep place into the *sea* (Mark 5:13). It was the *waterless* places in which the devils sought rest (Luke 11:24). A friend of mine, exploring the grounds of one of our oldest mental hospitals, reports that he found disused tanks in which, in earlier days, lunatics were thrown into deep water—a belt of cork with line attached having first been fitted—in an attempt to cure lunacy, which was often ascribed to demon possession. Note also our common phrase "between the devil and the deep sea."

[12] Luke 7:47.

to make us correct our own. I once had a letter from a policeman in which he paid a tribute to prostitutes. He wrote:

> In twenty-five years' service (thirteen in the East End of London) I never once met a Christian worker laboring among the real down-and-outs late at night or in the early hours. On the other hand I have often seen poor, bedraggled prostitutes "feeding up" some poor derelict at a coffee stall, not in any hope of gain, but out of sheer pity and goodness of heart. No wonder Jesus has a kind word and a promise for them.

How we turn up our noses at those who commit sins like stealing or forgery or drunkenness or the crimes of the criminal courts! We think that we should never even be tempted to commit them. It comes, surely, as a shock to realize that Christ is saying to us, "But you do things which are far worse." Our assessment is only that of society. His is that of God. It would do us no harm to realize that if sin were punished by society according to Christ's assessment of its wickedness, instead of that of society, we should all be in jail. For turning a man out of our pew, for stealing another's good name, for the kind of lying gossip common in most churches, for refusing to forgive or climb down and ask forgiveness, for confusing a little child's sense of values and making him to stumble, people would serve long sentences of penal servitude if sin were punished by society according to its sinfulness in the sight of God instead of in the sight of man.

2. "But," you say, "surely the woman's sin merited some condemnation. Wasn't it very dangerous for Jesus to say, 'Neither do I condemn thee'?"

Let us answer the question at once. There was no need for him to condemn her, for she already condemned herself. What is the object of condemnation? Surely to produce a sense of guilt, then of penitence, and thus to inaugurate a new beginning. The violence of the language of Jesus to the Pharisees was the measure of the thickness of the heavy armor they had constructed and behind which they complacently sheltered—the depth of the dugout beneath which they hid. They had no sense of guilt. They thought themselves the moral examples which all should emulate. In that lay their mortal peril. The woman had a burning and terrible sense of guilt. For one thing, as the Pharisees said, she was taken "in the very act." She could scarcely escape, then, a sense of guilt. For another, she was in the presence of the holiest of the sons of men. There was no need for Jesus to establish guilt. Further condemnation would have been unnecessary and cruel. It might have broken her and reduced her to hopelessness.

Some time ago the woman commandant of a large camp of women in the armed services asked me for an interview. Her story was that immorality was rife in the camp, but that when she gathered some of the worst girls and tried to make them behave better, the ringleader confronted her with the words of Christ which form our text. "If Christ didn't condemn this kind of thing," said the chief culprit, "surely you are not going to be more particular than he was. He didn't take immorality very seriously. Why should you?"

We can see through the plausible sophistry at once. The girls in the camp needed to be made to see just why and how immorality is evil; that it is not just convention, or the code of a polite society, that is broken, but that, apart from its effect on the lives of those who may be born from a lustful union, spiritually it is what our fathers called a way of death, and psychologically it is a certain road to ill health—psychological ill health and perhaps physical as well.

The woman in our story had advanced morally far beyond the standard of those girls. She had accepted the verdict of the most authoritative court in the world. Not a judgment of man, not even of God—for inasmuch as we often are not spiritually advanced enough to accept God's verdicts, they lack authority. The authority, as it were, goes over our heads. No, I mean the court of justice within our own hearts. I often think of the lines of Tennyson:

> [He] ever bears about
> A silent court of justice in his breast,
> Himself the judge and jury, and himself
> The prisoner at the bar.[13]

The only verdict that is of value is that which we pass on ourselves. The only punishment that has value to the one that suffers it is the discipline cheerfully accepted because it can make the sufferer what in his best moments he really wants to be.

It may be said, in passing, that the strongest argument against the doctrine of *everlasting* hell-fire is that the court of justice within the

[13] From "Sea Dreams."

human breast condemns everlasting suffering as unjust, whatever we may have done. If there is no chance of a new start, then punishment is robbed of its primary value. Even in human law the state punishes an offender, primarily not from the motive of retribution or to deter others, but from the motive of making him a useful member of society and calling forth from him a new effort to end his evil ways and contribute to the common good by expressing those good qualities which exist potentially in the most degraded.

If the punishment of hell were endless, it would defeat the end for which punishment exists. The sinner would have no chance to benefit by the punishment and begin again.

One other word about condemnation. Let us be slow to condemn others. Most of the people we meet in daily life are not hardened hypocrites demanding fierce words, nor do we stand where Christ stood, for we are probably hypocrites ourselves at some point or another.

Most of the folk we meet—unlike the Pharisees to whom Jesus spoke—think too little of themselves. They sin and they fail as we all do, but we can help them best by believing in the inherent good in man—as true a fact as that of original sin—and acting in a way that calls it forth.

We have one qualification for dealing with sinners that even Christ did not possess. We have been, and are, sinners ourselves. It is not as good a qualification as his sinlessness, but that is no reason why we should not use it. We are not to shout criticisms across a gulf which we shall make only wider, separating and estranging us from another. As Jung says, in a chapter which every minister should read, the last chapter of his book *Modern Man in Search of a Soul,* speaking of patients who certainly do not need to be made to feel they are sinners:

> Condemnation does not liberate, it oppresses. I am the oppressor of the person I condemn, not his friend and fellow sufferer. . . . Modern man has heard enough about guilt and sin. He is sorely beset by his own bad conscience and wants rather to learn how he is to reconcile himself with his own nature, how he is to love the enemy in his own heart and call the wolf his brother.[14]

In the private interview a psychologist must always learn to identify himself with the patient, walking along the same road with him, never

[14] Pp. 271, 274 (Kegan Paul).

condemning or being shocked, trying to understand how the patient got into the distress which troubles him. Any of us who tries to help another should say, in effect, "I cannot condemn you if I would, for I have erred in so many ways myself, but I can tell you of Jesus, who forgave and saved me; and I can show you the upward path which I am trying to follow."

> So let me draw you to the great Forgiveness,
> Not as one above who stoops to save you,
> Not as one who stands aside with counsel,
> Nay! as he who says, "I too was poisoned
> With the flowers that sting, but now, arisen,
> I am struggling up the path beside you;
> Rise and let us face these heights together."

3. Take one more look at Jesus and the woman he would not condemn. He bids her look at the future, not at the past. That is over and done with. "Go, and sin no more." That too is a message for most of us. When the High Court of Justice in our own breast has shown us how guilty we are, we may seek forgiveness and begin again. The court does not acquit us and make light of sin. It convicts us and passes a sentence, for sin carries consequences, and forgiveness does not remit them. But it does change them from the penalty of an impersonal, outraged, moral universe into the friendly discipline of a loving Father making us what he, and now what we, long for ourselves. But no looking back! Sin is "behind his back," "remembered against us no more," "as far from us as east from west, as heaven from earth." These are the gracious words of promise. We are to concentrate on the heights we are determined to attack, not look back into the depths in which we once wallowed. Christ's belief in us can even give us a picture of ourselves as he sees us—the picture that he can make a true one—and with that picture on the screen of our minds, with faith in him and in daily friendship with him, we can move forward. A friend told me recently of a beggar whose "pitch" was near the window of an artist's studio. From his window the artist painted the beggar and then called him in to see the portrait. The beggar did not recognize himself.

"Who is it?" he asked. And then, as recognition dawned, "Can it be me?" he asked incredulously.

"That is the man as I see him," said the artist.

The beggar made a sublime reply. "If that is the man you see," he said, "that is the man I will be."

If we could see ourselves as Christ sees us, we should not recognize ourselves, for he is able to "perfect that which concerneth [us]." [15] He who "hath begun a good work in [us] will perform it." [16] He already sees the men and women we can become by his grace. When he sent that poor woman away, he looked into her face and saw burning there the flame of purity "like a white candle in a holy place," for he had called up into consciousness and endued with new vitality and power the loveliness which at its best is synonymous with the word "womanhood." To us who have done worse things than the woman did, he says the same gracious word, giving us back a faith both in him and in ourselves. "Neither do I condemn thee; go, and sin no more."

[15] Ps. 138:8.
[16] Phil. 1:6.

IV

Is Any Sin Unpardonable?

HERE, AS RECORDED BY MARK, ARE THE WORDS WHICH HAVE CAUSED countless thousands to worry and fret:

> Verily I say unto you, all sins shall be forgiven unto the sons of men, and blasphemies wherewith soever they shall blaspheme: but he that shall blaspheme against the Holy Spirit hath never forgiveness, but is in danger of eternal damnation: because they said, He hath an unclean spirit.[1]

Matthew has a parallel passage which is just as difficult to explain:

> Wherefore I say unto you, all manner of sin and blasphemy shall be forgiven unto men: but the blasphemy against the Holy Ghost shall not be forgiven unto men. And whosoever speaketh against the Son of man, it shall be forgiven him: but whosoever speaketh against the Holy Ghost, it shall not be forgiven him, neither in this world, neither in the world to come.[2]

Naturally, people ask how there can be any sin which God refuses to forgive. They wonder what it means to sin against the Holy Spirit. Having been taught to believe in the Trinity, they cannot understand how a person can sin against the Holy Spirit in an unpardonable way without sinning against Christ in the same way. One of my correspondents says: "If we are to take Mark 3:29 literally, it is useless for a person to continue in the Christian faith once he is aware that he has committed the unpardonable sin." Many correspondents have written to the same effect.

The great trouble about this passage is that it is always the wrong people who worry about it, and these folk may be divided into two classes: (1) the very timid and sensitive people whose very timidity

[1] Mark 3:28-29.
[2] Matt. 12:31-32.

and sensitiveness make it impossible for them to have committed the unpardonable sin, and (2) the people who are psychologically ill. Anybody who works in a psychological clinic knows that every six months or so a distressed person will turn up who weeps in one's interview room and complains bitterly that there is no hope for him or her because the unpardonable sin has been committed and the despair of the damned has set in. I would warn any amateur who tries to deal with such a case that it is generally useless to attempt to comfort such a sufferer by asserting the loving forgiveness of God. The patient, generally a woman, says that that may be so for other people, but her case is hopeless, and with morbid insistence she reads out the passages above quoted and nothing that the amateur comforter can say or do can assuage the patient's grief, remove her despair, or persuade her that the unpardonable sin has not been committed. Such a patient generally needs psychological treatment. If I give you an actual case, it is only that you may see that matter clearly.

When analytical treatment had been applied to such a patient as I have described, it was found that as a young girl she had practiced masturbation. Her mother had discovered this—how she did so is not clear—and, thinking to break what is a bad habit rather than a sin (indeed, a habit which often is not a sin at all but a moral illness, requiring skilled psychological treatment rather than condemnation), told the patient that she had committed the unpardonable sin. This incident was "forgotten." It was pushed down into the unconscious part of the mind, but powerful feelings of guilt were still attached to it, and they rose into consciousness in the form of a terror—detached from the incident—that the unpardonable sin had been committed and that all hope was lost. The patient confessed that she found herself saying aloud such sentences as "Damn the Holy Ghost," and then being overcome with a panic-feeling of remorse and despair. The treatment consisted in recovering that early incident to the mind of the patient, removing from it the exaggerated sense of guilt attached to it, getting the patient to take a normal and sensible attitude to sex, whereupon the symptom of terror at having committed the unpardonable sin entirely disappeared. But let it be repeated, no argument would have succeeded, for arguments are received on the level of the *conscious* mind. The trouble lay far deeper in the unconscious mind to which the patient normally has no direct access, nor have the words of the would-be comforter.

Let us begin, therefore, by reminding anyone who tries to deal with people who say they have committed the unpardonable sin that sensitive people are incapable of committing it, and that psychological patients who say they have committed it must have sympathetic and competent treatment. I would underline this sentence in case anyone who is worrying about it should read these words. *If you are capable of worrying about it, you are incapable of committing it.*

Now let us look at the incident which lay behind the solemn language Jesus used. A man had been brought to Jesus who was blind and dumb, and Jesus healed him "insomuch that the dumb man both spake and saw." All the people were amazed and said, "Is not this the son of David?" But the Pharisees said, "This fellow doth not cast out devils, but by Beelzebub the prince of the devils."

In other words, here was an act of Jesus which, on any reading, was a good work. Any unbiased judgment would declare it good, but the vision of the Pharisees was so distorted by anger, fear, and hate that they called this good work evil. They called light darkness, and they tried to persuade others that an act which was obviously a good act was an evil act done by an evil man for an evil purpose.

Let us try to illustrate what a dreadful thing that is to do. In Mammoth Cave of Kentucky the waters in the farthest recesses of the cave are completely dark; the fish that swim there are quite blind. If such a fish is caught and examined, it is found that the structure of the eye is perfect, but the optic nerve is an insensate and shriveled thread. Having eyes, they see not. The eye can no longer carry the impulse of light and communicate it to the brain. The dread law of atrophy has been at work, the law by which the misuse or disuse of a faculty leads to the faculty's being withdrawn.

Now of course a fish cannot sin. It has no power of choice. But for the sake of the argument let us imagine for a moment that the fish swimming in the waters of those vast caves had the power to choose and that some deliberately chose to swim only in the dark water. Having chosen darkness, in a very little while such a fish could not distinguish between darkness and light. If later it swam out into the blazing light, it would call it darkness. If it were confronted with the blazing midday sun, it would be unconscious of the fact. It now knows no difference between midnight and noon. It has committed the unpardonable sin. It has so blunted its power to distinguish light from darkness that it calls light darkness, and it cannot regain its sight. It has so misused and disused the faculty of seeing that the power to see has perished.

This is a grim subject, but we must face the facts. The truth is that the same law runs through the spiritual world. If motivated by hatred or fear or anger, we begin to say, "This good is really evil. That good person is an evil person; his good deeds are evil deeds." If hate or any other motive of the devil does so completely possess us as to make us confuse light and darkness, we had better realize that we are heading slowly into those dark waters in which the power to distinguish light from darkness will be withdrawn. Such a person has committed the unpardonable sin. If he were confronted by the whole blaze of heaven and allowed to bask in the unmediated glory of God, it would be indistinguishable from the black darkness of hell. The anger and violence of Jesus are the measure of the greatness of the spiritual danger of the Pharisees. Malice and hate and jealousy and fear conspired together to turn them toward that darkness in which the highest faculty of the soul is lost, and their trick of talking to simple Galilean people so as to confuse *their* values—while it did not make those people commit the unpardonable sin—had led them into a mistaken attitude which might play havoc with their souls. They too would be blinded. They would not have committed the sin of blinding themselves, but the devilish trick of the Pharisees might lead them into the dim half-lights of uncertainty, whereas if they had been left to themselves, the glorious light that streamed from Christ and shone in all his works might have led them to see God in him and to rejoice.

In a day like this, when millions of people are hungry and when hundreds of thousands are literally starving, we can find an illustration that takes us part of the way. Let us imagine—and I only wish it were fact—that a company of us from the City Temple could go to a starving country with truckloads of nourishing food. Now imagine the little children with their pinched white faces and men and women with their gaunt frames rushing up to the trucks with arms outstretched. But then suppose a group of important people in a high, responsible, and authoritative position should come between the starving people and the trucks and shout to the people, "Don't touch it. It is poison! This is a trick to deceive you. Have nothing to do with this so-called food. These people are evil people on an evil errand." Then the starving might easily die.

The illustration, I think, goes a long way. Jesus, with his disciples, came bringing the very bread of life, the food of the soul, the nourishment which the soul needs to grow and develop so that it may ultimately be enabled to appreciate the glory of God and find its ultimate goal in perfect communion with him. The Pharisees, blinded by hate, shouted, "Don't touch it. It's poison! Have nothing to do with it. This man is of the devil." That is a sin without forgiveness.

Mark this carefully! It is not an unpardonable sin because God refuses to pardon it. There is no sin that anybody is capable of committing but he may find pardon for it if humbly he seeks such pardon from God, longs to be in a right relationship with God, and is ready to forgive his brother also and put his relationships with men as right as he can. But our illustrations go to show that the unpardonable sin is unpardonable because it leads a man into a situation where, through his own fault, he cannot discern what is sin. He has lost his power to distinguish between light and darkness, and therefore forgiveness is impossible. Man cannot be pardoned for a sin which he refuses to recognize as a sin. Concerning such a sin he is incapable of asking for pardon. His power to repent has gone. You remember those famous words of Shakespeare in *The Merchant of Venice:*

> The quality of mercy is not strain'd,
> It droppeth as the gentle rain from heaven
> Upon the place beneath. It is twice bless'd;
> It blesseth him that gives and him that takes.

But although the loving forgiveness of God falls as the gentle rain from heaven, it will not fall on tender plants if you have covered them all over with iron sheeting. God does not deny the rain, but you have put there something that keeps it from the plants. Similarly, God does not deny pardon to anyone, but if the tender growths of the soul are covered over with the sheet iron of a hardened conscience which keeps away from the soul that tender messenger of grace, then the unpardonable sin has been committed. Instead of a spirit sensitive to love and forgiveness, there is the hard shell of complacency and self-satisfaction.

If I were asked for a definition of the unpardonable sin, I should say that it is the sin of so continuously calling good evil that the power of discrimination is killed and therefore the power to repent and to flee from sin is lost. The hunger for God is inhibited. The soul cannot respond to light, for it knows no difference between light and darkness.

Another part of the question remains to be answered. If we believe in the Trinity, then surely sin against one Person is sin against all, and there can be no distinction which we can recognize as sin against the Holy Spirit. According to Matthew, Jesus said, "Whosoever speaketh a word against the Son of man, it shall be forgiven him: but whosoever speaketh against the Holy Spirit, it shall not be forgiven him." I have found no reference to this in the commentaries, but I have come to feel that Jesus means that he himself was capable of being misunderstood. While he was in the flesh, it was possible to misunderstand him. Some would mis-hear what he said. Some would hear only garbled accounts of his message. Indeed, even his own closest disciples misunderstood him again and again, and reacted accordingly. It is possible that a person might reject him and even turn against him on grounds that, however unfair to him, were based on misrepresentation. While Jesus was in the flesh, goodness was mediated through a human personality and, for a great majority, through the lips and doings of others.

But the Holy Spirit is within a man's own breast. It whispers to us again and again whenever there is a silence in the soul, and it says to us, without any possibility of misrepresentation, "That is wrong." To refuse that, to call that inner light darkness, is to silence that Spirit—a Spirit who will not always strive with man—and to make pardon, because it makes penitence, impossible.

A great many people will be comforted by what I have said so far. They will realize that at any rate they have not committed the unpardonable sin. But quite frankly I do think we should realize that for all of us there is a very solemn and, indeed, grim factor at work in the universe. If you like to put it so, there is a dark line in the face of God. The gospel is not all sunshine and flowers; there are facts in it that are as hard as rock, as unyielding as granite. I want Christianity to be as full of sunshine and flowers as Galilee is on a sunny day, but it would be a very poor pulpit ministry that made you imagine that God was what a Hyde Park orator called "soft mush," that he was sentimental and easy-going, even where our sins are concerned—that sin didn't matter much anyway, and that the idea of hell was an old-fashioned supersitition which nobody now took into his reckoning.

Recently a girl of seventeen wrote to me about a man of forty-two who made love to her. Day after day he made her feel that his whole heart was hers and that he only longed for her to accept him as her lover. She was young and blithe and happy, and had not thought very seriously of love, but gradually he won her heart until, as she says in her letter, her own interests faded out of the picture and she was interested only in him, what he promised and planned, and the vision of the wonderful things they were going to do together. She wrote, "I identified my life with his until all my interests were his, and then he snapped his fingers and laughed in my face, and actually introduced me to the girl he was going to marry, saying, 'You must have known all along that you were much too young for me.' " Then, amazingly, she added, "He doesn't think he has done anything wrong, and I must not blame him." Whether she blames him or not, whether he blames himself or not, there is no doubt that God blames him. If I said, "May God burn his soul in hell," it might sound unkind and unchristian, but I do say that. I do not believe for a moment that in his inmost heart he thinks he has done that young life no harm. He must surely know that he is a scoundrel, and he must know what he would feel if anyone else did that to his sister. But if he is light-hearted about it and thinks he can get away with it, I would say again, "May God burn his soul in hell," for that is ultimately the most loving thing to say. Left to himself he will swim into the dark waters and commit the unpardonable sin. His only hope is that he can be caught and challenged and turned round before the power to realize the sinfulness of sin is killed. Better that anything should happen to him than that; that any process of purgatory, however painful, should burn off the hardening shell with which he is covering his conscience than that he should be damned in an endless night.

Do not let us have a sloppy and sentimental Christianity that talks as if you can do what you like, that you can make hell of a young girl's life, and that you can get away with it and laugh at her and go your way with the next little bit of your fancy, and that nothing will ever happen to you. Let me say this very definitely. No one ever gets away with his sins. Every cause produces an effect. Even forgiveness does not cancel consequence, though it may change the terrifying penalty of what seems a soulless universe into the loving discipline of a Father. But everyone who sins must pass through the fire, and it depends on his attitude whether he perishes in it or whether he is cleansed by it. In my opinion we ourselves decide whether or not we turn purgatory into the complete destruction of hell or into the purifying discipline of a holy and loving God.

I am afraid we can find no easy and comfortable refuge from this, in the thought that God loves us. It is *because* he loves us that he makes us pass through the fires. It is *because* he believes that there is something to be saved "so as by fire" that, without first taking the most desperate measures to save what can be saved, he does not allow us to pass into the final destruction where probably men cease to be separate personalities at all.

I admit that the words about hell have been caricatured by our great-grandfathers until the picture in men's minds has been so dreadful, so unjust, so cruel, and so purposeless that they have thrown the whole idea away as though it were the superstition of a bygone age. But do remember that the most dreadful things that were said about sin were said by the gentlest lips in the world, the lips of Jesus, and that the idea of hell-fire, though it has been misstated, derives from the words of Jesus, and that no wangling with those words can ever deliver us from their grim intention. It was *Jesus* who spoke about the flame and the darkness and the closed door and the weeping and gnashing of teeth. God is not a sort of comfortable, good-natured old gentleman who will smile like a beneficent uncle on our birthday and, on the day of judgment, pat us on the back and say, "There, there, I am sure you didn't really mean to be wicked"! Sin is the most dreadful fact in the universe, and its greatest danger is that it blinds us to its own nature. As Martineau said: "It is the only thing in the universe which the more we practice it the less we understand its nature." We all recall the day we did something wrong and could not sleep for thinking about it and felt terribly ashamed and penitent concerning it, but we have so blinded our consciences that probably now we can do it twenty times a week without thinking about it at all. We have bandaged the eyes of our spirit, and unless God's loving mercy used every possible resource to strip the bandage from our eyes, we should lose our sight altogether. If you are not worrying about your sins, let me warn you that that is a bad symptom and shows an advanced state of disease and the possibility that you are on a road, the end of which is hell-fire, and unless, then, by your right reaction you turn hell-fire to purgatory—by which I mean you allow the fire to do its cleansing work, burn the rottenness and callous hardness away, and set your soul free to turn in penitence to God—then the ultimate end of that road is hell itself, which I presume is unending until personality disintegrates and is lost. It is clever and plausible to say that the loss of such a soul would be the failure of God and spoil the happiness of those in heaven, but it is no failure of God if the ultimate responsibility is on man. Even an omnipotent God cannot do self-contradictory actions. He cannot make a square circle. If it is one, it cannot be the other. God cannot make a man with a free will who is incapable of choosing evil. If he *cannot* choose evil, he is no longer a person with free will. In such a case even his "goodness" is without moral worth, since his power to be otherwise has vanished. He has ceased to be a real person at all unless his power to choose remains. Continuous choice of evil in the face of good, then, destroys the soul. And God has thus ordained matters. Not forever can the wicked blackmail the good and keep them from their happiness, nor must they be allowed, by their final refusal of good, to stain God's universe forever.

I sometimes find that people talk in the most slipshod way about the destinies of the human soul. You know the neighbor who leans over the garden wall on Sunday morning when you are just setting off for church and says, "Well, I am not a religious man. You must go your way, and I must go mine, but we are all going the same way really, and we all come to the same place." I do not want to be unneighborly, but I do not think we *are* on the same road, and I do not think we *shall* get to the same place. If your sensitiveness to God is increasing, you are going to heaven. If it is decreasing, you are on the road that leads to hell. Let me say again, you can change hell into purgatory as long as you have power to make response, but do not forget that sin, carelessly regarded and complacently viewed, is killing your power to make response. God will do everything in the world except use force to win you back, but he will not use force. He will have you because you choose him, and for no other reason. He will not disable your mental processes or inhibit your power to choose by a display of overwhelming might, or blind you with the glory of another world. As long as there is a spark, he can save you, but beware of a process which is slowly putting the fire out. Do you remember Browning?

> Beneath the veriest ash, there hides a spark of soul
> Which, quickened by love's breath, may yet pervade the whole
> O' the gray, and, free again, be fire.

Thank God there is infinite mercy and infinite hope while there is one spark that can be kindled by love's breath. But we should be very,

very foolish indeed to leave out the stern, dread note that runs through the shining pages of the New Testament, from which we are to learn that all humanity is divided into two classes, the people who say to God, "*Thy* will be done," and the people who insist on their own wrong way and cling to the darkness until it is indistinguishable from the light and to whom God in the end sorrowfully says, "*thy* will be done." The first are on the way to life, the life that is life indeed, the true life of heaven. The second are on their way to death. They pass into an experience that may be a fire that cleanses and saves; but if they insist on having it so, it will be a fire that devours them. The fire is not quenched. What they do in the fire determines their destiny.

V

Did Jesus Believe in Chance?

How often we wish people "good luck" and in the ordinary affairs of everyday life talk about our "good luck" or our "bad luck." Indeed, one of the bewildering facts of life is that, so often, immensely important happenings seem to turn on chance. Let us consider whether Jesus believed in chance, and what the Christian attitude is toward luck or accident.

A paragraph from a book by the late Archbishop of Canterbury, Dr. William Temple, reads:

> If when I am walking down the street a chimney-pot is blown down, hits me on the head and kills me, that does not prove that God decided to end my terrestrial existence on that day and took this means of doing so. The wind that knocked down the chimney-pot was due to causes traceable in the last resort to the nebula in which the solar system originated. The looseness of the chimney-pot was due (perhaps) to neglect on the part of a builder, which had its own moral explanation in his family history. My presence was due to my pursuit of my ordinary duties. No special act of God is involved except in so far as He did not work a miracle to save me when these three independent lines of causation converged to the production of the "accident." If there are to be general laws at all, there must be accidents, unless there is to be a miracle every time an accident would otherwise occur.[1]

I read in the press of a man who was copying his wife's guesses onto the form provided by the human vampires who arrange football pools. He made a slip and copied wrongly. But his wrong copy proved to be the right answer, and she won a small fortune. Isn't that chance?

For my own part I am quite sure that we must leave a place in our philosophy of life for what must be called "chance happenings" as long as we carefully define what we mean by such an expression.

[1] From *Christ the Truth,* p. 231. Copyright 1924 by The Macmillan Co. and used by their permission.

There cannot be such a thing as chance to God, because chance involves an unknown factor, and everything is known to God. A familiar illustration of chance or luck is the tossing up of a coin. We say that it is pure luck or chance whether it comes down heads or tails. But it is easy to realize that if we knew all the factors that are operating in the simple act of throwing up a coin—such as the weight of the coin, the resistance of the air, the energy expended in tossing it, the position of the coin when it left our fingers, and so on—we could work out scientifically how it would fall on the table or on the floor. It is because of the unknown factor that we speak of "the luck of the toss."

We need at the outset a definition. One dictionary calls luck "an undesigned occurrence"; another dictionary calls chance "an unforeseen event." But in view of our discussion, which is in the realm of religion, I suggest our definition be as follows: a chance happening is one that God did not intend and man could not foresee.

When I am asked whether Jesus believed in luck or chance or accident, I have to answer "Yes," because although I believe intensely in his divinity, I also believe just as intensely in his humanity. But I do not believe that—if I may put it thus—his divinity is to be subtracted from his humanity, or his humanity from his divinity. That is to say, he is not less divine because he is human and not less human because he is divine. Christian theologians remind us that, in becoming human, Christ renounced some of the attributes of a divine being, but not the essential of divinity.[2] Obviously he could not, while in the flesh, be omnipresent—present at all places at the same time—and I believe also that he renounced omniscience, or the power to know everything. No truly human person could know everything. He would not have to use faith and trust at all. Whereas the continual trust of Jesus in his Father is one of the qualities that attract us most. Further, no person who was omniscient could ever be surprised. Yet Jesus expressed surprise again and again. Indeed, Jesus said that there were things he did not know. "Of that day and that hour knoweth no man, . . . neither the Son, but the Father." [3] If, therefore, there were things he did not know, there must have been many events which, in the sense defined, were accidents, matters of chance or luck. He certainly did not believe that everything that happened was the direct intention of God—men's illnesses, for instance, for

[2] See Phil. 2:6-8.
[3] Mark 13:32.

he spoke of one patient as bound by *Satan*.[4] This element of luck does not obtrude much in the New Testament, but it is interesting that in one of Jesus' stories he used the word "chance." [5]

When we define chance or luck as an event which God did not intend and man cannot foresee, it seems to me important to guard against the idea that an event which God did not intend is altogether outside his will. The truth is that he *wills* that accidents shall be allowed to happen, but that does not mean that he intends them to happen. They are the product of the crisscross of streams of purpose which result from God's will. That is a difficult sentence which I must try to light up. Parents put their little child into the nursery. They do not cover the floor with eider downs or pad the walls. Therefore, when the little chap is trying to walk, he often falls and sometimes he hurts himself. They *allow* him to fall. They do not *intend* him to fall, or they would push him over. They allow, within the area of the nursery, a certain number of accidents which they do not intend and he cannot foresee. Hold on to that illustration because we shall come back to it later. In a similar way God allows sin, and it is within his will to allow sin, but he does not intend sin. Whenever we are thinking about God's ways with men, it is helpful to distinguish between those things which happen to us from God's direct intention and those things which happen to us because he allows them.

Superficial thinking might suggest that to believe in chance and luck is to disbelieve in the reign of law, but in truth this is not so. I believe most intensely that the universe is in every possible way a law-abiding system. Not only on the physical plane is this true, but on the mental and spiritual as well. This, please notice, does not deny miracles. Miracles happen. They are not denials of the reign of law, but illustrations, especially on the spiritual plane, of its scope, complexity, and wealth. It is incredible that at any point in the universe there is chaos. Everything is cosmos. Everything is order. Everything acts in response to law.

But, obviously, if those events which are the result of the activity of one law are impinged upon by events which are the result of another law at some point at which man enters, then, indeed, there may be an "accident" because God has ordained that man shall have a free will. And I know no better illustration of that than the one quoted already

[4] Luke 13:16.
[5] Luke 10:31.

from Archbishop Temple. The fact that the archbishop chose to walk along the road at that time made the subsequent event an accident.

I think we ought to realize that it is the purpose of God that man shall have free will; that he shall learn very, very slowly and in learning make mistakes; that he should be free to make a fool of himself; and that he should be free to sin. Those three things—sin, folly, and ignorance—are allowed by God, but not intended by him. It is his intention, indeed, to replace sin with holiness, folly with wisdom, and ignorance with knowledge; but while this replacement is slowly going on, ten thousand things can happen as the result of human sin or folly or ignorance which God did not intend and which man cannot foresee. Of this the fact of disease is a poignant illustration. It is not the *intention* of God. Jesus, who did his Father's will, always regarded illness as part of the kingdom of evil, and he fought it with all his power. Never let anyone hear you say about the illness of another, "It is the will of God." It is God's will to *allow* it while we fight and overcome those elements in the universe which are hostile to the happiness of man, but one day we shall thus overcome the germs of disease just as our great-grandfathers overcame the wolves that preyed on lonely rural folk. The pests now are smaller, but the problem is the same. And not now, preyed on by a thousand illnesses, but *then,* when they are conquered, we shall rightly declare, "This is the will of God."

Even though man stands in a law-abiding universe, yet since he is able to oppose the intention of those laws in the ways indicated, he can bring upon himself events which I think are best labeled as accident or luck or chance. They are not intended by God. They are not foreseeable by man. If man ever becomes the master over *all* the forces of the universe and at the same time is, indeed, a true child of God and one with the divine purpose, it is possible that he can to a great extent eliminate the element of luck. We note that the more he does control the universe and the more he does act in harmony with the intention of God, the more is chance excluded from his life.

At the same time, there are some events which take place, and sometimes with very disastrous consequences, for which neither man nor God can be blamed, and we have to label them simply "luck." I had an illustration of that on one occasion when I heard of a woman who was sleeping alone in a house one night and thought she heard a noise downstairs. She got out of bed and was moving toward the bedroom door, in order to open it and make investigations, when apparently the pressure of her feet on the floorboards of the bedroom disturbed the poise of a wardrobe. The door of the wardrobe, which had a mirror in it, swung open behind her. As she opened the bedroom door, the moving mirror in the wardrobe door reflected a beam of light that came in through the window from a street lamp. The reflected beam moved across the staircase as she opened the door, and she immediately thought the house had been invaded by burglars and that one of them was shining a light up the stairs from below. So terrified was she that she fainted and fell down the stairs. I think we certainly might call that an accident. Whose, indeed, was the fault? The man who fixed the floorboards or the man who made the wardrobe? Or was it stupid of the woman to be so afraid? But might not that fear go back to some childhood incident which was the fault of someone else? The matter becomes fantastic, and it is better to call such a thing an accident, for we may certainly say God did not intend it, and the poor woman certainly could not foresee it. The accident was *within* God's will. The laws that were operating concerning the reflection of light, the law of gravity, the swing of the wardrobe door, and so on were all his laws, but no one could say that it was God's fault the woman fell downstairs, or that the accident was his will in the sense that it was his intention. God is not that kind of person. "If ye then, being evil, know how to give good gifts unto your children, how much more shall your Father which is in heaven?" That was the argument Jesus used. God's intention is always our highest good. His laws are framed with that in mind. A chaotic absence of law would be calamitous indeed. We could never learn any of his ways. God's intervention and sudden holding up of his laws would be just as calamitous. It is certainly impossible for us to conceive any better basis on which a universe could be constructed. The very thought seems presumptuous.

A little while ago a nurse was cleaning a hypodermic syringe, pointing it upward. She was holding it by the barrel and working the piston, forgetting to hold the needle also. She was so energetic that the needle flew off and penetrated the eye of a brilliant surgeon who was an expert on microscopic work. He lost the sight of the eye which he used for his microscopic research. You blame the nurse? But of course she did not intend it. God did not intend it. Man could not foresee it. It was luck, chance, accident, due to man's folly impinging on the working of God's law-abiding system.

DID JESUS BELIEVE IN CHANCE?

We must now pass to another very difficult part of the argument.

Many people feel that if God knows everything, he knows that the so-called accident is going to happen, and therefore it must happen, and that this denies his good will toward us because he could ensure that his intention of good was carried out.

But in the first place it must be said that if we agree that the laws of the universe, laid down from its foundation, are in God's wisdom the best, then to cancel their action when what we have called an accident was imminent would deny his initial wisdom in laying those laws down. No accident happens which was unforeseen by him. He did not make the laws of the universe and then—when an accident was imminent—sit up in alarm and say, "I must work a miracle quickly. I never thought that such an accident could possibly happen."

Further, let us try to part once and for all from the heresy which supposes that if God knows a thing is going to happen, then *for that reason* it must happen. It is not God's knowing that makes a thing happen. It is the thing's happening that makes God know. I am sure we must try to separate in our minds the idea that because God knows—as he does—what is going to happen to you tomorrow, that knowing on the part of God is the thing which determines what shall happen. It is not so. Here is a girl who is about to sit for an examination, but she has not done an hour's honest work to prepare for it. I *know,* therefore, that she will fail, as of course God does. But it is not our knowing that makes her fail. It is her ignorance. If I hold out a lovely, juicy steak and someone admits a starving dog at a near-by door, I *know* that the dog will move toward the steak. But it is not my knowing that makes him move. It is his hunger. Similarly God knows what you are going to do with your free will tomorrow, but his knowing does not make it happen. Your power of choice makes it happen.

Further, although this again is a difficult thought for us to accept, the ideas of past, present, and future are concessions to our human limitations of apprehension. To God they are not in the same relationship as they are to us. To him everything exists in an eternal present, and it is just as true to say of an event that it *has* happened or *is* happening as it is to say that it *will* happen. Now, as we look back to the things of the past, we never assume that because God knows that they happened long ago his knowing made them happen. As we think of the things that are happening to us at the present moment, we do not assume that they are happening because

God knows they are happening. Why should we assume that the things in the future happen because God knows they will happen, when the verbs "happened," "are happening," and "will happen" all have the same meaning to him? I know that is a conception very hard to receive. The human mind is almost completely imprisoned within the barriers of time and space, but we must get out of our heads the idea of a fatalism based on a false view that because God knows the future, its events are determined by that fact.

But now we come to the most important point in my message. People may be inclined to say, "Well, I suppose life is just a matter of luck, and anything might happen." No! There you make a very great mistake. *Anything* cannot happen. I am quite sure of the most important fact that God has guarded this universe. Its laws are not infinite in number, and therefore only a certain number of possible things can happen. Of course I don't know what this number is. Nobody does. The permutations and combinations of all the possibilities that could happen on a planet governed by laws which God ordained are beyond the scope of man's mind. Perhaps if some brilliant supermathematician knew all the laws and all the possibilities, he could work out the sum, but by faith in the wisdom and love of God—not by any scientific guess—I am quite sure that there are only a certain number of things that can happen.

To see this, let us go back to the parable of the nursery. The parents who allow their child to stumble and fall in it as he learns to walk do not, we said, put eider downs on the floor and have the walls padded. In this way the child can get a nasty tumble. He can hurt himself fairly badly. *But the parents have excluded razor blades and bottles of sulphuric acid and arsenic*. In other words, they have guarded the nursery. It is not true to say that *anything* might happen. *Nothing can happen with which the child cannot cope as he learns to walk*. Nothing can happen from which he cannot win a definite gain. I believe that the whole environment of man is guarded by our loving Father in the same way. Some terrible things can happen, but it is not true to say that *anything* can happen. Nothing can possibly happen from which gain cannot be won. Nothing can possibly happen with which it is utterly beyond our powers to cope.

If a thing happens to you, therefore, God knows all about it. He knows it can happen, that it is going to happen, that it has happened. But he knows also that nothing can possibly happen in this nursery of a universe that of itself has power to defeat his own purposes, and that if man grasps his opportunities and uses his resources and seeks also his Father's aid—just as a child might stretch up a hand when he stumbles—real good can be won from everything that seems like unfortunate accident. From that fact a profound truth emerges to me: The apparent evil in any happening that *can* occur to man is the measure of God's challenge to man to transform it into advantage. It wouldn't be allowed if it could defeat God, just as razor blades and acid would not be allowed in a nursery by the most Spartan parent.

Look at it like this. Man is very proud of what he calls his scientific discoveries, and indeed they are tremendous. But from a religious point of view it is true to say that he can discover nothing unless God reveals it. What the scientist discovers God allows him to discover. The progress of the scientist's mind which allows him, benefiting from the discoveries of his predecessors, to startle the world with some new discovery is only an unveiling of one of the secrets of God by God himself, and man never made a discovery until he was in sight of power to cope with that discovery. If we could bring back our great-great-great-grandfathers and put them in the modern world, their sanity would be overturned. They would find that coping with the modern world was more than they could manage, for their minds would be utterly unattuned to its demands. Man has slowly climbed to his discoveries, and they have become discoveries only when he could use them for the happiness of his fellows and the glory of God. Yes, I know you are thinking of atomic energy. So am I. But don't let the horror of it disguise the fact that it *can* be used in man's service, even in his highest service. And here again the measure of the wonder of the discovery is God's challenge that it be used in his service. God is trusting us to use all new discoveries to further his plans.

So there are no accidents or chance happenings or bits of luck that are outside the scope of God's knowledge and man's power to deal with them adequately. Nothing can ever happen to us but in co-operation with God we can turn it into a spiritual gain. I mean that literally. Do not just meet the liability with an asset that is its equivalent, but turn the liability itself into an asset. So don't say, "Well, it's just a matter of luck, and all life is chance, and instead of purpose there are accidents." Remember the parable of the nursery. Nothing is allowed to happen that could ultimately defeat the purposes of God.

As I have thought about the problem of the place of chance in the

Christian life, I have found a kind of daydream taking shape in my mind. It has seemed to me as though a number of people were scattered through the length of a muddy lane, along which a laborer with a cart full of broken pieces of tile slowly passed, and to each person he gave a spadeful of fragments, which somehow the recipient knew he had to fit together into a pattern and the pattern into a pavement. In my dream many cried out to the laborer and said that of all those broken pieces of ill-assorted shapes and sizes they could make hardly any use at all, let alone make something beautiful. Then I saw in my dream that the more thoughtful people turned the fragments over, or exchanged some of theirs for others doled out to the people near them, and getting together made not only a beautiful pattern, but a firm pavement where there had been mud. It was a strange dream. The people who moved in its shadows complained loudly of injustice, for some got beautiful-colored stones, and these lucky people were able at once to make them into a pattern and set the pattern in the pavement. But others got rough-edged stones, dull of color, and they complained bitterly of their bad luck. But in my dream joy came to my heart when some of the most humble people who said nothing heard, as from an angel voice, the advice, "Turn them over!" and on doing so found they were holding precious stones.

I could not help feeling that somehow life is like that. This man has good luck, and that man has bad luck, but *I wonder whether, in the sight of God, there is any real difference between good luck and bad luck.* So often the latter is a frozen asset which ultimately brings immense spiritual wealth. Dives thought he had good luck and Lazarus bad, but in the next world things looked very different, and—if we *must* use time-words—we shall be longer there than here.[6] I would like you to think about that. Life cannot ultimately be unjust. I have seen the lucky ones finish their lives having made a very poor thing of their luck, and I have seen the unlucky ones turn the rough stones of ill luck over and find they were jewels, and turn the things we call calamities into a pattern of loveliness and a pathway for other feet. I think it is God's purpose that the lucky ones and the unlucky ones should make a pattern and a pavement, and cry out at last with Jeremy Taylor:

> Lord, come away;
> Why dost Thou stay?

[6] See Luke 16:19-31.

Thy road is ready and Thy paths made straight
With longing expectation wait
The consecration of Thy beauteous feet.

For "all things work together for good to them that love God," or, as C. H. Dodd translates the famous text, "With them that love Him, God co-operates, in all things, for good."

VI

Did Jesus Really Still a Storm?

And when they had sent away the multitude, they took him even as he was in the ship. And there were also with him other little ships. And there arose a great storm of wind, and the waves beat into the ship, so that it was now full. And he was in the hinder part of the ship, asleep on a pillow: and they awake him, and say unto him, Master, carest thou not that we perish? And he arose, and rebuked the wind, and said unto the sea, Peace, be still. And the wind ceased, and there was a great calm. And he said unto them, Why are ye so fearful? how is it that ye have no faith? And they feared exceedingly, and said one to another, What manner of man is this, that even the wind and the sea obey him?

—Mark 4:36-41

NO ONE MUST IMAGINE THAT IN WHAT I AM ABOUT TO SAY I AM denying the possibility of miracles. I believe in them. I accept, for example, the resurrection of Christ from the dead. It seems to me to be the foundation of Christianity. Nothing recognizable as New Testament Christianity is left if it is denied. I do not understand it. I cannot see how it is to be fitted into the views of the universe which the scientists have helped us to form.[1] But I cannot, for that reason, reject it. I am in no doubt that, whatever the means, it happened.

Similarly, in regard to the story of the stilling of the storm, I do not reject it because I regard it as impossible. One may say a thing is unlikely, but to say it is impossible one would have to be omniscient. Even if one knew all natural laws, there might be unknown exceptions, and this might be the case of the one exception. A beginner at physics might say that it is the law of nature that all things expand by being heated. But rubber contracts. He might say that cold increases the density of all objects, but at four degrees centigrade the density of cooling water suddenly decreases. Ice does not sink to the bottom of the pool, but floats on the top. The pond freezes from the top, not from the bottom, or the living creatures in it would perish.

[1] I have made some suggestions about this in the chapter on resurrection in *His Life and Ours* and in a little book *The Resurrection and the Life.*

Further, I accept the miracle of the Incarnation. I believe in the divinity of Christ. If these are accepted, belief in the possibility of Jesus' control of a storm is child's play.

At the same time I think it is a good rule to take the simpler explanation of any phenomenon rather than the supernatural or difficult, so long as the simpler explanation accounts for all the facts and does not leave anything out.

I think it is also true to the facts to say that *some* of the stories about Jesus, written down only long after the Ascension, in the course of being repeated by one to another and written and rewritten had the wonder element in them heightened. This is almost inevitable in the case of a beloved personality gradually, on other grounds, believed to be divine.

I have a strong and, I think, sincere feeling that our religious thought must be able to stand up to the facts of life. In these days especially, it is dangerous to have a religion which, while it may express itself in the deepest piety, is not intellectually sound. A false religion lets us down most grievously at those crises in our lives when we most wish that it were true.

The question which is most important to answer in regard to the story of Jesus in the storm on the Sea of Galilee is whether he said, "Peace, be still," to the waves or to the disciples. On our answer to that question depends a whole philosophy of life. Orthodox Christians up till comparatively recently believed that he spoke to the waves and that they obeyed him. This belief, in my opinion, is false. Not only is it false, but it is dangerous because it leads men to hope that religion can be used as an instrument to defend them and their beloved ones from those dangers in the world, whatever their source, to which all men are exposed.

For my own part I believe that when Jesus said, "Peace, be still," he was speaking to the men and not to the water. I know this appears unorthodox to many and may offend some, but so much hangs on it that we must look at the matter closely. Those who accept and share my own view do not expect religion to be any kind of safety device or insurance against danger, but they do expect religion to make all the difference to the way they react to those dangers that are involved in living on this dangerous earth.

Let me therefore quite briefly make six points which appear to me both important and relevant.

1. On a lovely summer morning in 1934 I was staying in Palestine on the shores of the Sea of Galilee and had arranged with some friends to go over to the other side of the lake to explore the "steep place" at which the pigs fell into the water.[2] The lake was as calm as a mirror when we sailed across it, and the sun was shining brightly from a cloudless sky. We had had nothing like the amount of time we desired for our exploration before our boatman came to us and said, "A storm will arise quickly. We ought to start back at once."

We looked up at the blue sky and down at the blue water, and, in the pride and arrogance of our British ignorance, we presumed to dictate to the boatman who had lived by the lake all his life. "Nonsense," we said. "A storm cannot possibly get up as quickly as that."

But he was so determined and so certain that, reluctantly and rather grumblingly, we got into the boat and started back toward Tiberias on the journey home. Before we had embarked more than a few moments, a storm arose which in a matter of a few minutes whipped up the water into waves so high as to make us distinctly uncomfortable; and an hour or so afterward, drenched to the skin with spray, wiser and sadder men and women, we disembarked. Yet before we had finished lunch, the lake looked as calm and innocent again as when we had set out.

Whether there are any other places on the earth's surface where this kind of thing happens, I do not know, but the Sea of Galilee is more than six hundred feet below sea level. The warm air from its surface rises quickly. The cold air from the snow-covered heights of Mount Hermon, which overshadows the lake, is funneled down the narrow gullies and wadis. And the effect on the water is similar to the effect of blowing on a basin of water with a pipette. In an incredibly short time a rough sea is produced, and in an equally incredibly short time peace is restored again.

This experience is spoken of by Basil Mathews in *The Life of Jesus*, where he says that in a few moments waves more than thirty feet high broke over the towers on the shore at Tiberias; and a traveler whose account is quoted in George Adam Smith's *Historical Geography of the Holy Land* says that at one moment the sea was calm and that within twenty minutes great waves were breaking and spray could be felt two

[2] Mark 5:13.

hundred yards from the shore.[3] If, then, we are to accept the view that the sudden cessation of the storm, related in Mark's Gospel, was due to the words of Jesus, what are we to make of the certain fact that sudden cessations of storms on the Sea of Galilee took place before Jesus' life and have taken place since, and that witnesses still living can testify to this fact?

2. Once grant the Incarnation, the fact that Jesus was the perfect manifestation of God in terms of a human life, and you are debarred, as I said earlier, from saying dogmatically what Jesus could do and what he could not do. But you are entitled to use your mind in regard to what is written about him and to ask: What is significant of him? What is like him? What constitutes a revelation of his Father's will? If we turn to John 5:19, we find a sentence attributed to Jesus which seems to me to be a key which gives us a clue to much of his activity: "The Son can do nothing of himself, but what he seeth the Father do." When Jesus was dealing with disease, he was putting right something that was wrong, and something that had been put wrong by human ignorance, human folly, or human sin. Since God is always trying to replace ignorance with knowledge, folly with wisdom, and sin with holiness, Jesus was obviously doing the will of God in fighting disease. But the case is not the same if Jesus altered the weather. We might argue that God's will is that man should be the master of nature and overcome its dangers by his courageous adventure and by adopting devices which his brain suggests and his hands invent. But if Jesus alters the weather at a word, since man cannot conceivably follow him in hushing thus the wind and the water, he is really criticizing those laws of God which permit storms. A storm on a lake, if it is evil, is not an evil wrought by man, but, unless the activity of devils is accepted, by God. This is impossible. Therefore to hush a storm with a word is certainly not the Son doing what he seeth the Father doing. It would be a case of the Son doing the opposite.

3. The third point that I want to make is based on another passage from the Fourth Gospel, where Jesus is reported to have said: "He that believeth on me, the works that I do shall he do also; and greater works

[3] Many travelers to Palestine have commented on these sudden storms and their cause. See W. M. Thomson, *The Land and the Book*, p. 375; Henry K. Booth, *The World of Jesus*, p. 104; Henry C. V. Morton, *In the Steps of the Master*, p. 96; James Hastings, ed., *Dictionary of the Bible*, p. 280.

than these shall he do; because I go unto my Father."[4] John had a wonderful insight into the nature of God because he had a wonderful insight into the nature of Jesus. And it is as though John is saying to us, "You must not misinterpret the miracles as though concerning them Jesus was saying, 'These I can do because of my divinity, but they must ever remain beyond you.'" John's picture of Jesus seems rather to reveal him as one who says concerning his miracles, "These are the activities of a man who is living in complete and perfect communion with God, and this is what God means you to do." The sooner we stop trying to prove the divinity of Christ from his miracles, the more truly shall we be reading our New Testament. Jesus' divinity is not proved by his ability to do things which other men cannot do. Jesus' divinity is proved by his moral character, his love, his knowledge of God, and his revelation of God's nature. Dr. Orchard once said, "If I saw somebody walking on the water, I should not say, 'This man is divine.' I should say, 'Excuse me, do you mind doing that again because I didn't see how you did it?'" There is no intentional irreverence there. The radio broadcasting companies have accomplished things just as wonderful as some of the miracles of Jesus, but I have never heard anyone claim that they are divine. As far as producing a sense of wonder goes, a modern scientist could impress a savage as much as Jesus impressed the disciples. But the scientist would not establish divinity thereby. So there is no loss in our estimate of the Master if we interpret some of his actions in a more humanistic way. Miracles are to be expected when a person like Jesus is operating. But it is not their magical quality which impresses me. It is the insight they give me into the nature of Jesus and of God.

4. The fourth point I want to make is that if you imagine Jesus as a perfect man—and that is to put the matter at its lowest—and then imagine that Man talking to inanimate things like wind and waves, other than in a completely poetical sense, you are committed to a view of the universe which is retrogressive. The Greek word that is used and translated "Be still" means literally "Be muzzled." Since the common people of Jesus' day thought that a storm was brought about by the activity of devils, when Mark came to write the story that Peter told him about Jesus in the storm, it was most natural that he should use that word. The word is used in Mark 1:25 for the casting out of a demon and is there translated, "Hold thy peace." But the word, or one like it, may

[4] John 14:12.

originally have been used to the men themselves, and some writers believe that it provides an illustration of Jesus' use of slang (other examples of which I have often noted), and that colloquially the word might be translated by our phrase "Shut up."

5. But the fifth thing I want to say about our story is the most important. I want to ask which is the greater, which is the more true to the nature of God as far as we can understand it, and which, therefore, is the more like Jesus—to ask for a faith which expects miracles, miracles which apparently involve the suspension of God's laws for the deliverance of the few favored ones, or a faith which believes that man can never fall out of God's arms even if he falls to the bottom of the sea?

The point is of enormous importance. Many of us have loved ones who are on the high seas. They are exposed to the dangers of storm and tempest. Are we to pray that because *our* loved ones are on board a certain ship, it may sail always on calm seas? If so, I cannot offer that prayer with any faith at all. Or are we to pray that our loved ones may have faith and courage so that whatever storms may roar without them, there may be peace and stillness in their hearts?

We cannot think too often of the brave men on the sea. Surely Christ is with them as truly as he was with men on the Sea of Galilee. Do let us have a religion that is bigger and truer and stronger than a faith steeped in credulity and magic which our great-grandfathers tried to hold because it seemed to them the only way of being loyal to the gospel story.

6. The sixth point that I want to make is that belief in miracles in the old-fashioned sense makes religion just the kind of insurance policy which Jesus said so definitely men ought not to hold. The traditionalist view of miracles asks us to imagine Jesus resorting to magic in order to work a sign that would dazzle his contemporaries and present their minds with evidence of his power which they had no means of examining or refuting. If one accepted the traditionalist view of miracles, one would be forced to conclude that, unable to get his message across on its own merits, Jesus resorted to dazzling tricks to prove his power and make an impression. One may be forgiven for saying that such a spirit is the spirit of blackmail. No one would dare to deny any claims that Jesus liked to make. If they did, he would resort to some miracle which would disable their argument. This is certainly the spirit which permeates some sections of the Old Testament where we are asked to believe

that if God was not obeyed, a woman might become a pillar of salt; if the ark was touched, the offender perished; if God's people were threatened, whole armies might magically be wiped out. Nothing could be further from the truth than that Jesus represented God to be that kind of person. Nothing is further from the truth than that he was that kind of person himself. The story of his temptations shows us how he put that thought of the abuse of power far from him, and again and again the Gospels make it clear to us how he often failed because he depended on human faith, was hindered by human ignorance, temporarily defeated by human sin, and that, with an awe-inspiring respect for the frailty of human hearts, there was room for men to deny him, and power in their hands sufficient to put him to death.

I know that if you turn to certain of the psalms, you can find support for the view of religion which supposes that God physically protects his own from danger. But do remember that some of those psalms were written hundreds of years before Christ. Some of them express the deepest aspirations of the human heart for God, but some of them incorporate an altogether false view of God. "A thousand shall fall at thy side, and ten thousand at thy right hand; but it shall not come nigh thee." [5] Jesus so definitely spoke in the opposite terms. "Ye shall be hated of all men for my name's sake." [6] "They shall lay their hands on you, and persecute you, delivering you up to the synagogues, and into prisons, being brought before kings and rulers for my name's sake." [7] But Jesus goes on to say, "It shall turn to you for a testimony." [8] And the end of Matthew's Gospel closes with the triumphant promise, "And lo, I am with you alway, even unto the end of the world." [9]

That is a religion I can work with. Never in the history of the world were men in greater need of a true religion that faces up to the facts of life at every point, and never lets them down. When the City Temple was burned down, some members of a church in London which shall be nameless joined together to sign a letter and sent it to my church secretary, pointing out to him that no wonder the City Temple had been burned down. They said it was the wrath of God, and that it was the direct consequence of my heretical preaching. When, a month later, their

[5] Ps. 91:7.
[6] Matt. 10:22.
[7] Luke 21:12.
[8] Luke 21:13.
[9] Matt. 28:20.

own church was also gutted by enemy bombs, there emanated from them a great silence!

"Be not afraid of them that kill the body, and after that have no more that they can do." [10] What a strong note is sounded there! How much finer is this than a religion that shelters the favored and the pious from the risks and dangers that confront other people! If we can go into the places of danger and death, not expecting that our prayers will effect deliverance, but knowing that the Master of life, who himself was not delivered from death, is with us, that there can be peace in our hearts whatever storms may roar about us, that we cannot fall out of God's arms, whatever happens; and if we can go with undismayed courage, with infectious cheerfulness, with contagious serenity, we shall not be among those who continually demand evidences of the power of religion and who seek a magic deliverance through their prayers. We shall be among those whose lives *are* evidences of the power of religion and who recommend their Master to others by the splendor of their own lives.

What happened on the lake, I think, was this. The little band went out with Jesus across the sea. "They took him even as he was," [11] says the rather pathetic phrase of Mark. He was tired and hungry. As we should say, "done up." He lay down in the stern of the ship. The Greek word translated "pillow" might mean a tiny cabin in the stern. Suddenly, as happened so often on the lake, a storm came up. They were afraid and also irritated. (After all, it is irritating to find that others can sleep when we are being kept awake!) "Don't you care that we perish?" they said, and he replied, "Peace! Be quiet!" Mark was writing about A.D. 60. The event happened about A.D. 27. We notice the time lag. We realize that in that interval those who wrote about Jesus and who loved him deeply would, without knowing it, "write him up," seek to make him yet more wonderful, never dreaming that unconsciously they were making claims for him that he himself repudiated. Peter thought Jesus was exorcising the demon who caused the storm, and Mark used the appropriate word. In Eph. 2:2 we find that the list of evil powers includes the prince of the power of the wind, the devil that causes storms. Peter thought Jesus was casting out this devil in order to calm the sea.

But the reproach in the voice of Jesus as he spoke to his men was the

[10] Luke 12:4.
[11] Mark 4:36.

reproach of one who so greatly wanted them to understand the true nature of God. He reproached them because the storm seemed nearer than God and bigger than God and more real than God, and more important than God. "Be quiet," he said to them, knowing that every man who shouted out, "Master, we perish," and who expressed the emotion of fear, spread that fear to another's heart and deepened it in his own. The urgency of Christ's voice was the measure of the danger lest others in the boat be infected by the faithlessness of those who spread abroad their terror.

We can learn the lesson of the story best when we go out into a world that is full of danger, knowing the peace of those who trust that God, who made the world and allows its terror, would not allow anything that of itself could tear us from his care. Let me quote to you an ancient prayer:

> Help us daily to know more of Thee, and through us, by the power of Thy spirit, show forth Thyself to others. Make us humble, brave and loving; make us ready for adventure. *We do not ask that Thou wilt keep us safe, but that Thou wilt keep us loyal:* Who for us didst face death unafraid, and dost live and reign for ever and ever.

"We do not ask that Thou wilt keep us safe." Yet we *are* safe after all. Listen to Rupert Brooke:

> War knows no power. Safe shall be my going,
> Secretly armed against all death's endeavour;
> Safe though all safety's lost; safe where men fall;
> And if these poor limbs die, safest of all.[12]

[12] From "Safety." Reprinted by permission of Dodd, Mead & Co. Copyright, 1915, by Dodd, Mead & Co.

VII

Did Jesus Really Curse a Fig Tree?

Now in the morning as he returned into the city, he hungered. And when he saw a fig tree in the way, he came to it, and found nothing thereon, but leaves only, and said unto it, Let no fruit grow on thee henceforward for ever. And presently the fig tree withered away. And when the disciples saw it, they marvelled, saying, How soon is the fig tree withered away! —Matt. 21:18-20

And on the morrow, when they were come from Bethany, he was hungry: and seeing a fig tree afar off having leaves, he came, if haply he might find any thing thereon: and when he came to it, he found nothing but leaves; for the time of figs was not yet. And Jesus answered and said unto it, No man eat fruit of thee hereafter for ever. And his disciples heard it. —Mark 11:12-14

He spake also this parable; A certain man had a fig tree planted in his vineyard; and he came and sought fruit thereon, and found none. Then said he unto the dresser of his vineyard, Behold, these three years I come seeking fruit on this fig tree, and find none: cut it down; why cumbereth it the ground? And he answering said unto him, Lord, let it alone this year also, till I shall dig about it, and dung it: and if it bear fruit, well: and if not, then after that thou shalt cut it down. —Luke 13:6-9

I SUPPOSE YOU HAVE HEARD ABOUT WHAT IS CALLED THE APOCRYPHAL Gospel of St. Thomas. It is a document which the authorities decided was not of sufficiently inspired quality to be included in what we call the Bible. It was rejected, to use their phraseology, from the "canon" of the New Testament. In that gospel there are some strange stories told. One of them describes the childhood of Jesus and relates an incident in which he is supposed to have made clay sparrows, and then touched them and made them fly away. We read another incident in which a playfellow pushed him over, and was cursed with leprosy forthwith. So strange and so repulsive are these stories to us that we reject them without stopping to ask the critics whether they are true or not, and in doing so we follow a rule which I think is a good one. That is to say, we make up our picture of Jesus from all the evidence we have, and if there is something that is entirely out of harmony with the great mass of that evidence, we reject it, or we as good as reject it. We say to ourselves, "I shall have to wait until I get more light on that." I suppose we all do that without thinking about it. If you read that Jesus said, "All that ever came before me are thieves and robbers," a passage which occurs in the Fourth Gospel, and then you think of Moses and Elijah and Isaiah and John the Baptist, you come to the conclusion, apart altogether from what scholars may say, either that Jesus never said that at all, or that he meant something by it other than the translation bleakly suggests. We judge the Bible by Jesus, not Jesus by the Bible, yet it is from the Bible we get what we believe to be a true picture of him.

I am concerned that you should notice that rule of interpretation. We have a certain picture of Jesus made up from the four Gospels and any other evidence we can collect from the authentic experiences of men. If there is something that does not harmonize with that picture, we put it on one side and say, "It cannot be true, or else there must be light upon it that explains it in some other way." I think that is a sound rule to adopt.

It may be that when you read this story of a man going from Bethany to Jerusalem who sees a fig tree covered with leaves, and who goes up to the tree, being hungry, as Mark says, and finds there are no figs on it and then curses the tree, so that it withers up, even though it is not the right season for figs, as the story says, you may decide that that is rather like the stories in the apocryphal Gospel of St. Thomas, and you may say to yourself, "It is so unlike Jesus that I simply don't believe it, and I shall leave it out." Frankly, I shall not criticize you if you come to that conclusion. The extraordinary thing about the Gospels is that there are so few pictures of our Lord that we cannot receive for this reason. But that is not the interpretation which I myself would like to offer you.

As I look up the authorities, I find that the point about its not being the season of the figs is got over in two ways. Shafto, who wrote a very useful book on the miracles, says that the fig tree has two crops in a year.

The first crop is the first-ripe fig mentioned in Isaiah (xxviii, 4) and in Hosea (ix, 10). It comes on the old wood at the same time as the leaf buds, and a fig tree in full leaf would have plenty. This first-ripe fig, so-called, is eaten by working people and is on sale in the poor quarters of Jerusalem. The second crop comes in August and is called the true crop.

That is very interesting. Bishop Gore refers to the knops, or buds, of the fig flower, which he says are the green figs of the Song of Songs and are commonly eaten and appear when the tree is in full leaf. That might account, think these scholars, for the strange assertion that Jesus went up looking for figs on the tree when it was not the season of the figs. But the main difficulty remains. Did he really address a tree and curse it, and did it really die, because such behavior *sounds* as petulant as a child stung with a nettle, cursing it or cutting it down with a stick.

I think there are two solutions to this problem. The first is that, of course, it may all have happened as indicated by the text of Mark's Gospel. If Jesus was, and is, the person orthodoxy asserts, if he is Lord of creation, if "all things were made by him; and without him was not any thing made that was made," it would be very presumptuous for me, or for any student of the New Testament, to say he could not possibly speak to a fig tree and make it die. Someone objects and says, "It is outside the law of nature." For myself I have become very hesitant about saying what is outside the law of nature. If Jesus is the Lord of nature, then what he determines *becomes* the nature of the creation.

That sounds like a rather difficult thing to me. Let me illustrate it like this. Someone might say to me, "You cannot make a burn on human flesh without something hot." Or, "You cannot produce a blister on the skin without either something hot or an acid." If I said, "But a blister can be produced on the skin by touching it with a pencil," the answer might be, "That is outside the law of nature." But it isn't. If a person is hypnotized deeply enough and told that the pencil of the hypnotist is a red-hot iron, then should the pencil touch the skin, a blister will follow because the mind in which the critical faculty is temporarily suspended has accepted the idea of being burned, and the physical phenomenon of the blister follows. Not only have I seen that happen, but I have done it myself under scientific conditions where the flesh has been bandaged and the bandage sealed, and the blister has been examined by adequate medical authorities and all other possibilities have been excluded. It is within the laws of nature that if the human mind, deep down, accepts an idea which is reasonable, that idea will come true.

Who are we to say that when a mind like the mind of Christ is in operation, a fig tree can withstand the energies that proceed from it? I think that to rule out this incident as quite impossible is altogether too presumptuous. It is not very wise or clever to say, "I have never seen this happen," or, "I can't see how this could happen, therefore it is quite impossible."

But look! That third lesson in Luke gives the whole incident as if it were a parable. "He spake also this parable." For my own part I am inclined to think that Luke got this story from sources other than the sources used by Matthew and Mark, and that he recorded it as a parable. A parable need not, of course, be an actual incident.

You may say then, "Well, how has it become an incident in Mark's version?" I can only introduce you to the very interesting fact that Jewish teachers were very fond of dramatizing their parables by action in a way that sounds almost ludicrous to us. When Isaiah was prophesying the doom that he felt was falling upon Israel, when he believed that the land would be stripped by its enemies and made naked, he went about naked. When they saw this strange, unclad figure moving about, they said, "What on earth is he doing?" and those with insight said, "He is prophesying the nakedness of the land." How unforgettable would such a message be!

In the same way, when Micah was prophesying the humiliation that he felt was going to fall upon Israel, he rolled himself about in the mud, in order to draw attention to his message. He did not just preach a sermon which people would forget. If I rolled about in the mud, it would be reported in the *Evening Standard* tomorrow: "Preacher rolls in the mud." And many, no doubt, would make comment, "Quite right, too; that's the place for him." But with complete sincerity and with complete naturalness Eastern and Palestinian prophets dramatized their message in that way.

In the same way Jeremiah, when he was prophesying that Israel would fall under the tyranny of another nation, went about wearing an enormous yoke round his neck, the kind of yoke that they put on the necks of oxen—an unforgettable sermon. How impressive it must have been! He was dramatizing his message.

In the same way John the Baptist dressed himself as Elijah, clothed himself in camel's hair and fed on the locust bean of the wilderness and cried upon men to repent, so that they said, "Is this Elijah come back again?"

In a small way the disciples did the same sort of thing as all Easterners did. They took off their sandals and shook the dust off them when they departed from a village that had annoyed them. We read of people shaving their heads and rending their garments. We have forgotten that kind of thing to a large extent. We do it here and there in little ways. We do it every day in one way when we shake hands with somebody. It is a dramatic action. It meant originally, "See, I have no weapon in my hand. I am not concealing a dagger. You can hold my hand and prove that I am your friend." That kind of dramatic action is slipping away from the West. What is important is that it was very common in the East and is easily missed by the Western reader.

Our Lord, you will remember, did that kind of thing himself. He washed the disciples' feet, a dramatic action illustrating the lesson of humility and probably far more than that. He rode on a donkey into Jerusalem, another dramatic action which those who knew their Old Testament would readily interpret. After that, in a most sacred moment, he gave them broken bread and poured-out wine, not just bread and wine—*broken* bread and *poured-out* wine—and said, "This means my body broken for you, and this means my blood poured out for you. Do this, break your body [not just do this, eat it and drink it]. Do this, break your body, if necessary, for my sake; pour out your blood, if necessary, for me. Give yourself wholly to me." So we call it the Sacrament. The *sacramentum* was the Roman soldier's oath of allegiance that he would follow the orders of his captain until death. That service means a thousand things, and I will not dilate on them now, but it began with the broken bread and the poured-out wine of a dramatic parable.

Let us, in the light of all this, look at the story of the fig tree. Remember the onslaught of Jesus on the religion of the Pharisees. Remember how deeply he was stirred by the way they misrepresented religion. He has made the word "Pharisee" a reproach ever since by the way he used it. If we call somebody a "Pharisee," we are calling him a hypocrite. There were, no doubt, some dear old gentlemen among the Pharisees, but to Jesus it was intolerable that, through the Pharisees, the word "religion" —which ought to light up the human mind as "springtime" or "dawn" or "love" or "bird song" lights it up—should light up the mind with ideas of tyranny and burdens and ceremonials and endless prayers. And he was determined to hit false religion hard, and said, "Look at that fig tree, all leaves and no fruit! Let it be cursed!" —*not meaning the tree, but the religion of which it was a picture,* the thing that produced a profusion and show and could not feed the hunger of one man passing on the dusty road from Bethany to Jerusalem.

I do not myself believe that Jesus was the kind of person who would curse a tree, this Christ of beauty who loved the flowers and praised the trees. But when he saw all those leaves and could not find even those first-ripe figs or the flower buds eaten by the poor, when he found nothing but a great show of leaves, he cursed *the thing of which it is a picture.* The situation offered him a dramatic parable such as his soul reveled in.

Obviously if he could use that tree to remind those who were listening to him of the futility of a religion that is pretense, that is just the kind of thing that he would do. Tradition says—I don't know what there is in it—that for years on the road between Bethany and Jerusalem there was an old gnarled, withered tree, and men said, "That is the tree that Jesus cursed." Whether they took some tree that had died and hitched that tradition on to it, I don't know. I don't think it matters. Believe what seems to you the natural explanation. If I am asked, "Did the tree really die?" I don't know. But I think we have in the fig tree story a dramatized parable used by one who pointed to something that was all show and had no real sustaining fruit on it, and cursed that of which it was a picture, the false and pretentious religion which has no reality about it.

If that is so, if we are to take it that way as a parable, then the most important thing we can do is to make sure that we have got hold of the lesson Jesus was trying to teach.

Let me talk now of that awesome note that runs through history. You hear it sounded again and again. You see a great civilization rise, and then you see it fall and disappear. Thus pass away the civilizations which God can no longer use.

You imagine the psalmist sitting down under the trees in Babylon, and you think of "Babylon the mighty." The words were a slogan of the day. Babylon was a far more pretentious civilization in some senses than ours. And you imagine that handful of Jews. If you had said to one of the proud legislators of that Babylonian epoch, "Well, what is going to happen to this little body of Jews whom you have brought into captivity?" you can imagine the answer, "They are just a handful of slaves. They will become incorporated in the life of Babylon. They will be absorbed by us." But history has judged between them!

You think of another civilization like Greece, boasting its great names—Plato, Aristotle, and the rest—and you think of a little crippled man on Mars Hill at Athens. He did not come from any of the great schools that Greece recognized, and he stood up on Mars Hill. He had a trained mind all right, but I don't think he had a very good time that day, preaching on Mars Hill. In the account in the book of Acts you can see, in imagination, the curl of the lips of these Greek philosophers as they look at this little fellow, and say, "What does he think he is telling us about? He comes to the land of Plato with the story of a crucified Carpenter!" And they laugh at him and sneer him out of their city. But history has judged between them!

You think of the great empire of Rome and imagine Pilate standing there with all the authority of world-wide, all-conquering Rome, and you see a Prisoner standing before him, with a pale face and deep-set eyes, wearing a crown of thorns, a Leader deserted by even his own followers. And you hear Pilate say, "Knowest thou not that I have power to crucify thee? Answerest thou me nothing?" And there is a gentle voice that says, "Thou wouldst have no power at all against me were it not given thee from my Father." And the crowds outside are shouting, "Away with him! Crucify him! Why waste time with this deserted revolutionary in the presence of the immense and august might of imperial Rome? Away with him!" And Pilate went to bed that night and thought, "That is the end of another Jewish rising." But history has judged between them! Pilate would never have been heard of but for his Prisoner.

And behold the Western world of today, with American wealth and British prestige! But right through history, and through the words of the Master, there is an ominous note, as though there were a hand knocking at the door of the Assembly of the United Nations, which rules the West, and if the door is opened half an inch, there is a Voice speaking. Don't you feel a little bit afraid that the door may be slammed, that we may say, "It isn't practical politics. We can't deal with that"? All right! I keep on reminding myself of the Breton fishermen's proverb: "He that will not heed the helm shall heed the rocks." I keep on reminding myself of the cynical remark of a great teacher: "The only lesson that history teaches is that men will not learn the lesson that history teaches."

I should be failing you very badly if I left out the note of doom that runs right through the New Testament. I should be failing you very, very badly if I did not remind you that if Christ is indeed the Son of God, and if his words are not false, and if the New Testament is not a delusion, and if the lives of the saints are not records of neurotic disease; if, by any chance, he is right, then any policy that moves away from him instead of toward him is leading whoever follows it to destruction.

I would like to end with two short prayers. The first is this: "O God, let not our beloved land fail thee. Make it the instrument of thy purposes in the world." And the second little prayer is this: "O God, help me to love thee, not merely with my feelings, but with my mind and my will, so that in word and deed, without pretense and without show, I may be thy child, obedient and loving, unselfish and responsive, every day."

What a mighty tree this Western civilization has grown to be! What a show of leaves! But if the Master finds it fruitless, its doom is certain.

VIII

Did Jesus Praise a Grafter?

If there is one story of Jesus which has caused more controversy than any other, I should think it is the story of the unjust steward, recorded only by Luke (16:1-13). It sounds as though Jesus told a story of a grafter and not only commended the grafter, but added, "Make to yourselves friends of the mammon of unrighteousness." Here is the story:

> And he said also unto his disciples, There was a certain rich man, which had a steward; and the same was accused unto him that he had wasted his goods. And he called him, and said to him, How is it that I hear this of thee? give an account of thy stewardship; for thou mayest be no longer steward. Then the steward said within himself, what shall I do? for my lord taketh away from me the stewardship: I cannot dig; to beg I am ashamed. I am resolved what to do, that, when I am put out of the stewardship, they may receive me into their houses. So he called every one of his lord's debtors unto him, and said unto the first, How much owest thou unto my lord? And he said, An hundred measures of oil. And he said unto him, Take thy bill, and sit down quickly, and write fifty. Then said he to another, And how much owest thou? And he said, An hundred measures of wheat. And he said unto him, Take thy bill and write fourscore. And the lord commended the unjust steward, because he had done wisely: for the children of this world are in their generation wiser than the children of light. And I say unto you, Make to yourselves friends of the mammon of unrighteousness; that, when ye fail, they may receive you into everlasting habitations. He that is faithful in that which is least is faithful also in much: and he that is unjust in the least is unjust in much. If therefore ye have not been faithful in the unrighteous mammon, who will commit to your trust the true riches? And if ye have not been faithful in that which is another man's, who shall give you that which is your own? No servant can serve two masters: for either he will hate the one, and love the other; or else he will hold to the one, and despise the other. Ye cannot serve God and mammon.

Let's put the story in our own modern way. Here is a Jewish merchant, who, by the rules of his own religion, is not allowed to engage in lending out goods for gain. Usury was condemned by all his moral teachers,[1]

[1] See Exod. 22:25; Lev. 25:36; Deut. 23:19; Ps. 15:5.

though the Jews practice it more than any other race and it is an accepted principle now throughout the whole world. So in the story this Jew appoints a non-Jewish steward, or agent, who would lend, say, a quantity of seed belonging to his master to some farmer or tenant who was either very poor or who had had a bad harvest the previous year, and then at harvesttime count on getting back a larger quantity of seed, part of which would go to his master and part to himself.

One day the steward, or agent, wakes up to find himself threatened with dismissal. He is given his notice. Note the basis of the charge against the steward. He is not sacked for dishonesty. The whole business is dishonest, and the "boss" is as dishonest as his agent. No, the charge against the agent is that he wasted his master's goods. What probably happened was that he so overcharged the interest that a borrower threatened to complain to the boss and call off the deal, or take it to court. To keep the borrower quiet, the agent probably gave him presents from his master's stores, but in the end the borrower reported him and the charge against him was that he wasted his master's goods.[2]

The agent's outlook is bleak. "I have no strength to dig," he says, "and to beg I am ashamed." He certainly could not have been a very popular figure in a community which knew him for a moneylender who squeezed as much as he could out of his customers by exploiting their times of need and distress. If he does get the sack, it looks as if he will not have a roof over his head.

Then he gets a brain wave (the Greek word [3] could well be translated "I've got it!"). He calls a customer.

"You owe a hundred measures of oil?"

"Yes."

"Here is a new agreement. We'll call it fifty."

He calls another.

"You owe a hundred measures of wheat?"

"Yes."

"Call it eighty."

What a grafter!

But note, he wasn't robbing his master by doing that. We know that because we are told (vs. 8), "The lord commended the unjust steward."

[2] Alfred Plummer, *Luke* (International Critical Commentary), p. 382.
[3] ἔγνων.

What he was cutting down was his *own* rake-off. And he did it for two reasons: one was a last desperate effort to keep the customer from going to the boss and calling off the whole deal. If the customer had gone to court, the boss would have lost his case and with it his loan of oil or wheat. An agent who charges so much commission that the customer calls off the deal or threatens proceedings is a waster fit only for dismissal. This waster saved the transaction just in time by having the foresight to cut down his own commission. The second reason was that if the agent *did* get the sack, he would, at any rate, have a few friends who were under an obligation to him and who would be kind to him. He looked ahead.[4] Moffatt translates: "The master praised the dishonest factor for looking ahead; for the children of this world look further ahead, in dealing with their own generation, than the children of Light."

Before we take up the phrase about making "friends of the mammon of unrighteousness," let's clear our thought so far.

Jesus tells a story which might well be a true incident. We are not to regard it as an allegory. It is absurd to put this story in the same category as the parable of the prodigal son in the previous chapter. There you may liken God to the father in the story and the modern penitent to the prodigal. But *here* you must not argue that God is like the moneylender and that the Christian should act as the agent, for the moneylender was a knave and the agent a grafter. We note that Jesus did not preface this story with the usual phrase, "The kingdom of heaven is like . . ."

At the same time we can approve the foresight and shrewdness of a villain without approving his villainy. We all admire, in the modern thriller, the resourcefulness of the crook without approving his crooked ways.

Jesus admired and praised foresight and ingenuity, resourcefulness and quick, decisive action. You are to be as wise as serpents,[5] he says. He condemned Dives for thinking of only his present fun. If he had looked ahead, he would have been happier in the "everlasting habitations."[6] He praised the virgins who remembered to buy oil in advance of

[4] Compare our Lord's praise for a man who looked ahead with the words "Take therefore no thought for the morrow" (Matt. 6:34). The literal interpretation of these words is in contradiction with the message of the parable of the unjust steward. "Take no thought" must be translated "Don't be so worried." Jesus always praised the man who looked ahead. Cf. Luke 14:28-32.

[5] Matt. 10:16. Note how pleased he was with a woman's resourceful answer in Mark 7:28.

[6] Cf. Luke 16:19-31 and 16:9.

the wedding feast; the man who thought out the cost of a tower beforehand; the man who built on the difficult rock, not on the easy sand, because he foresaw the storm; the man who had the foresight to sell all that he had and buy a field because treasure was hidden in it.

I take Jesus to mean, then, that the children of light, or, as he calls them elsewhere, the sons of the kingdom, ought to look ahead and use their brains as well in the service of God as the "sons of this world" do in order to do their business and obtain material security. If a grafter when in a hole can think clearly, plan ahead, and act resourcefully in his own interests, then he is to be commended to the religious man, who should not sit down and bemoan that "the will of God" has overtaken him—a piece of canting humbug—or wait for God to come to his aid, but in God's name rise up and show thoughtful, clear-headed planning, and resort to guided and bold action in the cause of the kingdom.

Especially should the religious man do what the agent did, forego present gain to make sure of future security. Let a man look ahead—as the agent did and Dives did not— and make sure that he is not imperiling the future by self-indulgence in the present. Jesus says, "Let a man use his present possessions by laying up treasure in heaven by means of them."

So now we come to that strange phrase, "Make to yourselves friends of the mammon of unrighteousness; that, when ye fail, they [the friends] may receive you into everlasting habitations."

What is the mammon of unrighteousness? Well, mammon we can take to mean money, in the personified way in which we say, "Money talks." [7]

It is important to understand that the phrase "the mammon of unrighteousness" does *not* mean money unrighteously gained.

Turn, for a moment, to the phrase in the twenty-third psalm, "the paths of righteousness." I have shown in another place [8] that that phrase means "a true path," a path that brings you out where you want to get, a path that fulfills the true purpose of a path. A path of unrighteousness would be a path that led, say, to a precipice or a swamp or just petered out in the jungle.

[7] Cf. G. R. H. Shafto, *Stories of the Kingdom*. Professor J. A. Findlay (*British Weekly*, October 21, 1943) thinks that mammon may have been the name of a heathen deity and does not merely represent money, but all kinds of perishable goods, like health, time, talents, and so on. But I leave the word "money" in the text. In any case money is a useful tangible representation of all kinds of material wealth.

[8] *A Shepherd Remembers*, pp. 93 ff.

Similarly, the mammon of righteousness would mean true wealth, wealth that brought something worth while. The mammon of unrighteousness means wealth that is deceptive, that does not buy the worthwhile and lasting things, assets which lose their value. The best phrase I can think of is "temporal" or "perishing" money.[9] The "mammon of unrighteousness" does not imply that money is evil. In itself it is amoral, but it is fleeting and temporary, and its value passes away.

What, then, is Jesus saying? Here is a paraphrase. "Here is this rascal of an agent who has at least enough sense to look ahead. He realizes that if he clings to his commission, he will lose his job. So he parts with present gain to make sure of future security. You should do the same. Don't you, who are 'children of the light,' show less foresight than a 'son of this world'! Use the wealth that perishes to show kindness to those around you. Then, when you die and your money won't buy you anything, you will find awaiting you the people you were kind to, the folk you put on their feet. And though money perishes and is no use after death, kindness goes on, and the people you've befriended will welcome you in the life beyond. That's a much better way of investing your money than anything you can do with it on earth, for that kind of investment brings dividends payable after death and dividends that go on forever.

"Don't use your wealth in such a silly way that when you pass into another world you find it has done nothing for you. Remember 'a shroud has no pocket in it.' 'We brought nothing into this world, and it is certain we can carry nothing out.' Invest in friendship. Make to yourselves friends by means of this perishing wealth, so that when it fails and can purchase nothing for you, those friends who have been put under obligation to you by your kindness to them will receive you into the courts of heaven. Thus you will change the 'mammon of unrighteousness'—the deceptive wealth that will buy only material things—into the mammon of righteousness, the true wealth that buys things that last forever. The things seen are temporal. The things like kindness, which are unseen, are eternal."

I am rewriting these words at a time when the message of Jesus seems singularly appropriate. How *shall* we invest our money? Gone are the

[9] I have borrowed the translation "perishing money" from an article written in the *British Weekly* (June 16, 1920) by the late David Smith in response to a reader's inquiry as to the meaning of "mammon of unrighteousness."

days of economic security. Most people under modern conditions cannot possibly save enough and invest in such a way as to make certain of an old age free from anxiety.

That grafter of an agent was wise in more ways than one. Not only did he hit on a ruse (cutting down his commission) which would probably mean the cancellation of his dismissal notice; not only did he take steps to put people under obligation to help him materially if he did get the sack; but he realized two very great truths. The first is that to have friends is better than to have material advantages, and the second is that it is worth losing present advantages to make sure of future security.

I had an interesting confirmation of the former in an earlier ministry. A man and his wife had lived and worked hard in Leeds for many years. They had saved up and were eager to retire and live at Bournemouth. At last the day came to retire. On their last Sunday in Leeds they came to my vestry after the service to say good-by. They were as excited as children. They had got themselves a lovely house. It had all the labor-saving devices so dear to the heart of a woman. I remember how thrilled she was at the thought of a stainless steel sink! From some of the windows, by screwing your neck round, you could actually get a glimpse of the sea! I said good-by and off they went.

But three months later I saw the man in Leeds. "What are you doing?" I asked.

"Looking for a house," said he.

"Looking for a house?" I was incredulous. "But I thought . . ."

He interrupted, speaking intensely and quickly. "It was awful," he said. "No one ever called. It was November when we arrived. The sea looked so depressing I couldn't bear the sight of it. Day after day cold winds, driving rain, and that gray, gray sea. But *it was the friends we missed*. Why, here if I go to town I nearly always see someone I know, and they greet me, and friends drop in and I go to see them. . . ."

He had saved up all his life for a fine house, and then he found that *his investments in friendship were the only ones that paid him the kind of dividend he wanted most of all*. Yes, it's one of the things you learn when you get older. Friends are better than any material wealth or even nature's beauty.

Jesus says that investing in friendship is the only way of using wealth in this world so that it will pay a dividend in the other. He does not mean, of course, that you can buy friends with money, but you can use the wealth that perishes in such a way, by doing kind things with it, that you will have the gratitude of people forever.

I remember reading of a queer dream. In his dream a rich man went to heaven and was being shown round the shining streets and the homes —some of them of many mansions. At last they came to a very small and squalid dwelling. "This is yours," said the angel—and then, catching the look of disappointment on the rich man's face, he added, "You did not give us enough material to build anything better."

The poets say these things better than we do. Listen to Percy Ainsworth:

> The only heaven thou shalt behold
> Is builded of thy thoughts and deeds,
> Hopes are its pearls and faith its gold,
> And love is all the light it needs.[10]

And then listen to John Masefield:

> And he who gives a child a treat
> Makes joy-bells ring in Heaven's street,
> And he who gives a child a home
> Builds palaces in Kingdom come.[11]

"Lay up for yourselves treasures in heaven," says Jesus, "where neither moth nor rust doth corrupt, and where thieves do not break through nor steal." "Use your temporary, material wealth," he says, in the passage we have studied, "to do so many kind deeds that, when you pass to where money has no meaning, grateful hearts will break the loneliness of dying and receive you into the eternal city."

Nothing, then, in this world or the next, pays like kindness. No investment pays a dividend to compare with that. When you reach the next world, would you like the angels to nudge one another and say, "Here comes old Jones. By slaving hard all his life he has saved a small fortune"? Or would you not rather hear our Lord say, "Inasmuch as ye have done it unto one of the least of these my brethren, ye have done it unto me"?

[10] From "The Kingdom Within." Used by permission The Epworth Press, holder of copyright.
[11] From "The Everlasting Mercy." Copyright 1911 by John Masefield. Used by permission of The Macmillan Co.

IX

Did Jesus Disapprove of Wealth?

THE SUBJECT OF THE CHRISTIAN ATTITUDE TO WEALTH MAY SEEM TO many to be irrelevant in that the heavy taxation of these days has almost made the rich man—in the old-fashioned sense—an extinct species.

About that I would make two comments.

The first is that all of us are wealthy in comparison with the Indian coolie who lives in a mud hut and gets only a few cents a day. Many of us are wealthy compared with the very poor of our great cities.

The second is that a faulty attitude to wealth is observable not only among those who possess it, but among those who covet it. Like every minister, I go into homes where things seen are worshiped and into homes where things unseen are worshiped, but that division is not a division between the rich and the poor. I know some rich folk who have never been lured from their ideals by the "deceitfulness of riches," and I know some poor people who are resentful and bitter because they are poor and who would do almost anything to achieve riches. The measure of a poor man's resentment is often the measure of a greater greed than the richly-born ever feel.

To consider, then, the Christian attitude to money is incumbent upon all of us. We all have to deal with it; and if we regarded it not merely as the equivalent of material possessions, but as a convenient way of translating service to the community into a tangible means of exchange, we should be willing to think about it with a greater sense of responsibility. In parenthesis, those who have inherited money or win it by gambling should try to remember that somebody worked for it. Every piece represents the labor of someone's hands and head. There is no such thing as a lady or gentleman of independent means. As for betting, there are many arguments against it, but one is that it is taking money out of the community which does not represent service given to it, and a form of trifling with the labor-equivalent of other men's brains and hands.

It is commonly supposed that Christ was a poor man, and that he praised poor men and condemned the rich; that Christianity regards poverty as a high virtue and wealth as under suspicion, if not under condemnation. Let us look at this.

Many passages, like the Magnificat ("The rich he hath sent empty away"), support this view, but actually Christ was not a poor man in any extreme sense. He was first a hard-working carpenter and then the head of a traveling band of preachers. Such traveling bands were frequently financed by a group of wealthy women in Jerusalem.[1] Judas, we are told, was the treasurer and carried the bag. Presumably there was money in the bag. Jesus did not have to worry where the next meal was coming from; and when he said he had not where to lay his head, I feel certain he meant to imply not abject poverty, but uncertainty of movement; that he had no settled abode, none of the apparent security of a house of his own, and that the disciples must be ready to travel. Many homes would have opened to him and been proud to give him a place to lay his head. His clothes were not rags like those of Lazarus the beggar. He wore such beautiful clothes that when the soldiers on Calvary stripped him they would not divide such lovely garments, but cast lots for them.[2]

Further, Jesus was undoubtedly entertained in the homes of rich men like Zacchæus and Simon, for example; and he ate the Last Supper in a "large upper room furnished." He could not have done this consistently if wealth was in itself an evil thing. For to accept the hospitality of the rich without comment is inconsistent for one who believes that the possession of riches is wicked.

I am not trying to prove that Jesus was what we call well off. But I see no evidence in the Gospels either that he was hampered by personal poverty, or that he condemned the wealth of others. He told the rich young ruler to sell all and give to the poor because, *in the ruler's case,* it was his money that was strangling his soul. We are not at liberty to take one sentence, spoken to one man in one special set of circumstances, as if it applied to all men in all circumstances. Francis of Assisi, one feels sure, felt that God was asking him to renounce his wealth. But Jesus often

[1] See Luke 8:2-3; Acts 13:50.
[2] John 19:23-24.

praised Abraham, who was one of the richest men of whom the Bible speaks. In the parable of the talents Jesus praised the man who traded to make five talents into ten. He once praised a woman who spent "three hundred pence" on scent and poured it over his feet, and in doing so he said, "You've always got the poor with you. You haven't always got me." [3]

No one, I feel, can really quote Christ in favor of remaining needlessly poor, certainly not of being lazy and covering laziness with the plea that poverty is a Christian virtue. No one can find Christian support for leaving one's loved ones to the charity of others. I knew a minister who left a fortune, and certain newspapers made a sarcastic comment. But he did far more good in the world than most poor men have done. A lot of cant is talked on this subject, and sometimes the rich are made to feel lonely. A woman once complained that her minister never visited her, and added, "You can't get any personal spiritual help in this parish unless you are poor or ill."

Jesus, I feel, moved among people and saw them as individual persons, apart from their possessions or lack of them. He would never, we can be sure, patronize the poor or flatter the rich, but would regard their possessions as bulking far less large than we would.

It is difficult, of course, to define words like "rich" and "poor." I should call a man rich who can afford luxuries, and a man poor who cannot afford necessities, though that definition still leaves unsettled what luxuries and necessities are!

We can clear our thought about money by making some observations.

1. *A Christian must earn honestly.* Does he crush others to make money for himself? I knew a case where the director of a vast system of chain stores ousted the village grocer by underselling, until the grocer was ruined, and then prices were put up higher than the grocer's prices had been. A man in a business run on dishonest or on cutthroat competitive lines has many conscience problems to face which I have no right or ability to answer for him, but I think Jesus would say that it is better to get into a job with a lower salary than sell your soul to an unscrupulous firm for a high wage.

Can we show Christ all our books? Can we claim his approval for the ways in which our money is made? Listen to Jesus: "If thy hand or thy foot offend thee, cut them off, and cast them from thee: it is better for

[3] Mark 14:7.

thee to enter into life halt or maimed, rather than having two hands or two feet to be cast into everlasting fire." In other words, if your job (the thing you do with your hands) or the path you are treading (the direction your feet take) leads to the loss of your hold on eternal values, cut it out whatever the cost. "And if thine eye offend thee, pluck it out, and cast it from thee: it is better for thee to enter into life with one eye, rather than having two eyes to be cast into hell fire." Isn't it better to live a "one-eyed life" than to "see life" and lose your soul? "What shall it profit a man, if he shall gain the whole world, and lose his own soul?" [4]

2. *A Christian must spend wisely.* Our great-grandfathers used to give one tenth of their income to God. No one can dictate to another about this, but I think the Christian should scrutinize his giving. What is his motive in piling up material possessions? Does his desire to spend run up into the realm of those values which belong to the kingdom of heaven or down to those values which belong to the kingdom of earth?

As to charity, it is certainly not right that within the fellowship of the church some should dwell in luxury while others lack necessities. To give to the poor is certainly in line with our Lord's will. But the difficulties are so great that no one can generalize. It must be part of the church's duty to eradicate the *causes* of extreme poverty, for merely to relieve it, though valuable, is to treat the symptom and not the disease.

3. *A Christian should save altruistically.* His own old age should not be an unnecessary burden on others. And his dear ones, or those who have served him for many years, are entitled to have provision made for them. Jesus could ignore these questions, but in this matter we are unlike him, and I cannot think it is his will that men should allow others to feel unnecessarily destitute and insecure in the evening of their lives. The education of children, again, is surely a legitimate demand on us. It is a better contribution to society, in my view, to educate children so that they are equipped to serve the community, rather than to give the money away to the community, and better for the child to be given a first-class education, through which he may express his personality, than to leave him a lot of money. To contribute thus to the life of the community is better for both parties than to depend on it.

When all that is said, it cannot be denied that the New Testament witnesses eloquently and repeatedly to the dangers of making money. Look at some of these dangers.

[4] Mark 8:36. See especially Matt. 18:8.

1. *The danger of false security.* Perhaps the rich young ruler was in that danger. "They that are whole," said Jesus, "have no need of a physician." We might make up a similar saying thus: "People who say they have no need of anything will believe that they have no need of God." Money, especially if accompanied by health and happiness, can produce the illusion that it can buy anything and that all difficulties can be overcome by it. But it cannot. Rich people are certainly no happier than the poor. Generally the reverse.

2. *The danger of getting our sense of values wrong.* Jenny Lind, the great Swedish soprano, disappointed many of her friends because she turned down so many big contracts that would have made her world famous. One day a friend surprised her sitting on a sunny seashore reading the New Testament. The friend, in conversation, rebuked the singer for not seizing her chances. Quickly Jenny Lind put her hand over her Testament and said, "I found that making vast sums of money was spoiling my taste for this." You need a strong personality to make a decision like that, but it's the right one. If we don't watch it, our money will get our sense of values distorted. Hoarding gold, if one may still symbolically use the phrase, is harming us if we are so obsessed by it that we no longer thrill to the golden glory of a cornfield or the golden splendor of the setting sun, if the light on a goldfinch's wing moves us not, if a field of golden buttercups leaves us cold, if both brain and fingers itch to get hold of money and neither can be rested by the aureole of golden hair round the head of a little child. "The love of money," as Paul said to Timothy, "is the root of all evil." [5]

There's a lovely legend about the pipe on which Moses played when he was a shepherd. It is said that the pipe was handed down and handed down, and became a very precious thing indeed. At length the pipe which the lips of the great Moses had touched was thought to be too valuable to be left in its crude form, so they covered it with gold, but then *it could not be played.* Its commercial value was enhanced, but its real value had gone. It could no longer do what it was fashioned to do. Gold can do that for us.

Two clergymen watched a great ecclesiastical procession pass, with silver incense lamps and priests wearing cloth of gold. As a great golden crucifix was carried past them, one said to the other, "The church cannot say now, as Peter said, 'Silver and gold have I none.' "

[5] I Tim. 6:10.

Instantly the other replied, "No, and neither can the church say what Peter said, 'In the name of Jesus Christ of Nazareth rise up and walk.' "

We have lost our power.

3. *The danger of making us selfish.* You would think it would have the opposite effect—that a man would say when he had made a bit of money, "Now I can afford to be generous." But the facts are that, in proportion to what they possess, the poor give incomparably better than the rich. Money makes you afraid you'll lose it. It makes you want to get just a bit more.

Look through a glass window and you see others, men and women and children, outside. Look into a so-called looking glass and you see only yourself. Ah! there is *silver* behind the second. It's an old parable, but its message is true. Wealth does not help us to see the needs of others. It hinders us. Silver can stop the vision of the needs of others. It makes us look at ourselves with pathetic introspection and wonder whether we have made enough to keep us safe in a world where there is no safety left, and no security save the love of God.

Perhaps it was for these reasons that Jesus spoke so sadly, "With what difficulty shall they that put their trust in riches enter into the kingdom of heaven. Easier is it for a thick cable to pass through the eye of a needle than for a rich man to enter into the kingdom of heaven." [6]

4. *The danger of drugging the conscience.* The fourth danger of wealth is that it makes men treat the poor with patronage. Instead of finding and removing the causes of poverty, rich men buy with money the gratitude of the poor, as an anodyne for their own consciences. Charity can do as much harm to the recipient as to the donor. "It is more blessed to give than to receive," we quote. But the true saying is always quoted to emphasize the blessedness of giving, never the curse of having to receive. It is not the curse of poverty but of being patronized. It is terrible for a self-respecting man to have to receive from the community and be denied by a rotten social setup from being able to give to the community in return. To use money to express friendliness is excellent, but to misuse money to drug one's conscience is bad. It is wrong that a man's

[6] I feel sure Jesus was too great an artist to mix a metaphor. He did not say it was easier for a camel to pass through the eye of a needle, and the pretty story that a gate into Jerusalem was called Needle's Eye Gate is, I am afraid, fictitious. The Greek word for "camel" is *camelos* and for "cable" is *camilos,* and the copyist has mistaken the one for the other. This I am certain is the explanation of what is, in any case, an Eastern poetic exaggeration. Both are obviously impossible if the words are mistakenly taken literally.

money can buy him a gratitude that makes him lazy and complacent concerning the task of ending the causes of dire poverty.

No equality of income is possible since the gifts and initiative of men vary so much, but the vast disparity of wealth and poverty could be lessened and ought to be. Money is power, and, as we are tired of hearing, power corrupts. It often corrupts those who have it and corrupts those on whom it is spent.

I think our closing word must be that wealth in itself is an amoral force. It is like electricity, which can be used to light a brothel or light a church.

A man who becomes rich is like a man who exchanges a bicycle for a powerful car. A car can be very useful. You can do a lot more good work with a car than with a bicycle. You can give others a lift along the dusty road. But you are a far more dangerous person. You can injure others and land yourself in the ditch, hurt even to death.

So it is with money. If you are a dedicated person, your money can be an extension of your personality, an increase to the range of your influence. You can do an immense amount of good with it, and give many a poor traveler a lift by the wayside. Baxter, in *The Christian Directory,* says, "If God shows you a way in which you may lawfully get more than in another way (without wrong to your soul or to any other), if you refuse this and choose the less gainful way, you cross one of the ends of your calling and you refuse to be God's steward." Big business can be an expression of religious aspiration. As the Bishop of Birmingham (Dr. Barnes) said: "There is no more reason why the businessman should put money-making before social service, than that the lawyer should put money-making before justice."

But it is a dangerous business. You may lose your head over it; you may hurt others with it, even your dear ones, by taking away their own independence and incentives. And you can certainly land yourself in the ditch with it, and a ditch so deep that many a man has never climbed out. Money suffocated him.

Note the inwardness of some of the phrases men use about money-making. They say he made a living. Yes, but did he live? When he dies, they say his net personalty was worth so much. Ah! but what was his net personality worth? They say he was *worth* so much money. Is that all? They say he *left* so much money. What did he take with him, and what, in terms other than cash, did he leave behind? They say he *made* so much money. Did he make so much as one little child happy?

What do you really want most? Isn't it life? Really to have lived. Fullness of life. It is an odd thing that so often the angel told by God to look after us whispers in our ear the words of the highwayman in the old thriller, "Your money or your life."

If you are challenged like that, do choose *life*. Jesus did not say, "I am come that they might make money." He said, "I am come that they might have life."

Salem - 3/11/51

X

Can a Christian Be a Communist?

If communism were a political creed reconcilable with Christianity, it would be no part of the job of the Christian minister to speak about it from the pulpit, where no one can easily challenge what he says or make reply to his arguments. If communism is not reconcilable with Christianity, if a man cannot be at the same time a thorough communist and a good Christian, if the two are fundamentally incompatible, then the Christian minister ought to speak about it as powerfully as he can, for several reasons.

1. Communism is not a force that we can ignore. It threatens now the whole of Europe and is ruthless, widespread, and powerful. It is the second most challenging idea in the world and the only serious rival to Christianity. It is believed in by 200,000,000 people covering one fifth of the earth's surface.

2. It is foolish to shrug the shoulders as though communism was merely an extension of socialism. Some people imagine that communism is an extreme form of socialism. In fact, it is something very different, for socialism believes that the state is a means and man an end, and that the state should exist to make man happy. But, as we shall see later, communism makes the state the end, and, quite frankly, if it succeeds, it will sweep away most of the freedoms which we now hold precious, and it will end all private property in terms of land or stocks and shares. If you lived in a communist country, you would be allowed to spend your wages in any way you liked, save that of buying land or stocks and shares. You would not be allowed to possess any capital or call a bit of land your own.

3. The third reason why the preacher ought to speak about it is that it is so foolish for some of us to talk about "those awful communists," without knowing what their creed is or why it is dangerous.

Let us begin by noticing some admirable things about communism.

1. The first is that, after all, it arose as a protest against the hardships of the unprivileged. I suppose it would be fair to date communism from the day the famous Communist Manifesto was published in 1847 by Karl Marx and Friedrich Engels. They were both Germans who came to England—Marx to London, Engels to Manchester—and their manifesto stated their new science of government. Considered as a protest, it was justifiable in the sense that it sought to remove definite evils, and it had the admirable motive of the welfare of the entire community.

Many people believe in capitalism. It is important to remember that capitalism also began as a similar protest. In 1789, through the influence of the French Revolution, capitalism arose as a protest against the vested interests and trade monopolies of the nobles. Once again, as with communism, capitalism as a protest was justified.

In all fairness, however, it is important to notice that capitalism has, in many ways, proved hostile to Christianity. This system has been misused to make the few wealthy and the many poor. It has been exploited to put power into the hands of the few, involving an unethical subjugation of the many. It has been misused until cutthroat competition and selfish ambition, rather than the service of the whole community, have been the outstanding motives. Yet it is very important to say that capitalism is not in essence this. It is not a system which in itself is necessarily a denial of Christianity. In the hands of some great Christians known to me personally I think that it is an interpretation of industry as close to the New Testament ideals as socialism. Into this matter we cannot now go.

What I am trying to say is that we must not start with a prejudice against communism, but we must remember that it was as sincere a protest against the treatment of unprivileged people as the capitalism which preceded it.

The Christian ought to begin with a bias in favor of any movement which protests against the unfair treatment of the poor, for surely Christianity is itself such a protest. The words of the "Red Flag" are not more revolutionary than the Magnificat. Listen to this: "He hath put down the mighty from their seats, and exalted them of low degree. He hath filled the hungry with good things; and the rich he hath sent empty away." [1] And what is the following passage from the New Testament but idealistic communism? "All that believed were together, and had

[1] Luke 1:52-53.

all things common; and they sold their possessions and goods, and parted them to all men, as every man had need." [2] Surely you could not find any stronger Christian support than that for the communist slogan, "From each according to his abilities, to each according to his needs."

Indeed, I make bold to say that within the fellowship of the church it is certainly unethical that one man should wallow in luxury if another fellow Christian in the same fellowship, after careful consideration by that fellowship, is left without necessities in a state of real poverty and need which is no fault of his own. Quite definitely, in my opinion, Christian progress must move toward the ideal that was originally behind the ideal of capitalism, communism, socialism, and Christianity.

2. Here is a second way in which communism claims our admiration. It is quite different from nazism, which was damned from the very start by its exclusive way of embracing only people of one blood or one race, the so-called *Herrenfolk*. Fascism was damned from the start, from our point of view, because of its exclusiveness in embracing only one state. Now, communism stands out quite distinctly from both nazism and fascism because it aims at producing a world society. It is to be a classless society in which everybody shares the amenities of life. As we should put it, everybody is to have an equal opportunity of sharing in the good gifts of God. These differences are important. Nazism is incompatible with Christianity, for you cannot be a nazi unless you have the right blood in your veins. The fascist system is incompatible with Christianity because, unless you belong to the right state, you are shut out from its benefits, even if you live within it. Communism is, at any rate, world-wide, and you are able to join the communist party whatever the color of your skin or the quality of the blood in your veins. Indeed, communism seeks to embrace the whole world. We may regard this—and, I think, ought to—as a menace, but at any rate communism is not exclusive.

3. The devotion of many communists also claims our admiration. Mind, we cannot possibly admire a creed which is pressed upon another with a violence that excludes him from even considering the claims of other ideologies, but I find, in my own heart, an admiration for some young people who have found a cause which, rightly or wrongly, they believe is going to make the world a happy and warless place, and they have devoted themselves to it with a readiness to sacrifice themselves to the very uttermost, and even to lay down their lives.

[2] Acts 2:44-45.

I could not help thinking that it was a compliment to communist influence to withdraw communists from civil service posts. The thought that they were such powerful missionaries that they were likely to change the constitution of any organism of which they were part is a compliment which I fear the modern Christian would not deserve. I was reminded of the early Methodists. There was a time when the aristocracy would not employ a Methodist cook, for she would seek to convert the housemaid and the kitchenmaid and the parlormaid and the between-maid, and spend and be spent in the activity. I am afraid that even a person hostile to Christianity would not hesitate to employ a member of any denomination today on the ground of his religious enthusiasm. Let us give credit where credit is due. A student is put down by the communist party in a university, and he is given the names of twenty-five other students, and he is pledged to win them to communism. If he does not do so, the communist party wants to know why. There are not many Christian students in our universities with the same degree of missionary ardor. We may criticize the methods used and realize what a nuisance to their fellow students such enthusiasts may be, but sometimes one wishes that the Christian fire was burning with the same intensity in the hearts of our Christian young people.

The communists have what they call "cells"—little groups of people pledged to attract others to themselves and enlarge the group. It is almost exactly Christ's idea of the leaven in the dough changing the quality of the whole, and I think we who believe in Christ have something to learn from this enthusiasm.

How, then, is communism irreconcilable with Christianity?

1. It leaves out God. The highest "value" in communism is material well-being. The spiritual is excluded. History is interpreted economically, never spiritually. We must refer constantly to Russia, because in no other country has communism been so widely and passionately tried out. In Russia the government is officially atheistic. A friend of mine who visited Russia told me that during the war people thronged the churches, unable to bear the deprivation of love and consolation in the hour of bereavement and anguish. Public opinion forced the authorities to open the churches and allow services of worship. But the government frowned on the phenomenon and met it in many places with countermeasures, such as the anti-God societies and the ridicule poured on some of the most sacred expressions of Christianity, such as the communion service.

No! Communism has no place for God, or for the forgiveness of sin, or for a divine purpose in history, or for a life after death, or for a living Christ, or even a moral life. A man can live a thoroughly immoral life and at the same time be a good communist.

2. The methods of communism have shown themselves to be those of force, violence, torture, and even murder. The communist will turn round when we say this and challenge us with war, which he regards as murder in the mass. The rebuke hurts, but even so there has never, in all history, until the rise of the nazis, been anything so utterly brutal as the methods the communists used in the Russian Revolution, and, indeed, the methods which are still in use if one is to believe one tenth of the statements in Kravchenko's dreadful indictment of communism, called *I Chose Freedom.*

3. The end of communism is the state. Man is only a means to that end. So long as the end is achieved, what happens to the means does not matter. There, of course, is a fundamental incongruity with Christianity. The record of the Christian Church has been smeared in the past by infamous persecutions and the irremovable stain of the Inquisition, but even so Christianity has never let go the ideal that man is an end because he is a child of God, that the end of all life is the glory of God, and that the highest well-being of man is an expression of that glory. Communism regards the state as the highest end; and if any of man's so-called rights or freedoms stand in the way, they are simply swept aside. His liberties of press or pulpit expression, his freedom to teach his faith to others, his freedom to vote, to live where he likes, to determine his own work, to read what paper he likes and listen in to what news he likes, his choice of books, the education of his children, and even his friendships are all restricted. Communism alone must be served, and to reach that end his freedoms are sacrificed.

Further, the penalties for indulging in any of those freedoms contrary to the direction given him are so horrible and ruthless that his life is lived in an unending and impenetrable atmosphere of terror.

4. Christianity has always held that the health of the state depends on the health of the family, which is the unit in the state. Communism does not hesitate to break up the family. Children are taken from parents. Husbands are directed to labor in mines and forests, and their wives do not even know where they are. Misery in Russia is as widespread as it was in the time of the czars, and the reigning force is a materialistic, godless

police state, with more than fifteen million people engaged in slave labor, and the whole country is governed by probably less than a dozen real rulers with incredible power in their hands.

In other words Lenin (1870-1924), who was supposed to have worked out a science of government capable of dealing with any situation and producing nation-wide happiness, has landed the country which he truly loved, and which still idolizes him, into a morass of misery, cruelty, and terror.

5. Christianity also believes in a world state, but Christianity seeks to establish it by man's free choice based on his insight into spiritual values, his acceptance of God as Father of all men and man as his brother and spiritual equal, to whom he is committed to show unbreakable good will. Communism, in seeking its world state of happiness, works by the method of forcibly changing man's outward environment, falsely hoping that the change of environment will change the man. As we have seen in the experiment, the most precious values in human life are sacrificed. In other words, communism just does not work. Christianity has not yet been tried with the influence behind it which communism has known, but where it is tried it is found that man's highest values are respected and his highest powers enabled to function for the enrichment of the whole community.

Ideally the Christian not only holds the unit of the family in immense respect as the fundamental unit in the state. He also regards the human family created by God as the model for the larger family we call the community, then the still larger family which we call the state, then the still larger family which I hope we shall one day know as the United Free States of Europe, and then the largest family of all, the world. The Christian seeks to work toward a goal which is a world family of God's children. In such a family all men are equal spiritually, just as all brothers in a family are equal spiritually. But just as the brothers in a family are unequal in terms of cultural development, education, qualities of leadership, and so on, so the Christian realizes that God himself is responsible for a certain inequality of man. You don't give your little brother a sharp tool, or a dangerous explosive, or ask him to do research with poisons, or to manage a business. At the same time, you never treat him in an unbrotherly way. He is equal on the plane of the brotherhood of man, but not necessarily equal in his ability or development. It must be so both in industry and in the world. Some men can lead; other men follow. Some have insights that immediately make them leaders of men. Others could not be such leaders. All should have equal opportunity, but it is impossible that all should hold equal responsibility. All should have access to sufficient property to enrich their own personality by its possession, but none should hold property in such an exclusive way that the personality of another brother, even a little brother, is deprived by that fact. Certainly no brothers ought to be in such need that the development of their own personality, or that of those dependent on them, is restricted by that need. I am in entire sympathy with the communist slogan, for it is true in every ideal family. "From each according to his abilities, to each according to his needs."

Clearly, two systems as different as this cannot mix. Russia has chosen communism. We ought to try to understand Russia. We ought to pray for Russia; and if any way opens to us, we ought, in a brotherly way, to try to show Russia what we believe to be a better way. More than this we cannot now do, but we cannot view with indifference Russian propaganda, or the communist attempt to spread across the world a way of life that is hostile to the spirit of Christ. To submit to the communist way of life would be not only to betray the dead who in two world wars died for liberty, but to deny Christ, who died to unite the whole world in one great brotherhood of mankind.

Yet I think we must realize that the spirit and threat of communism challenge us all, and I think the challenge is threefold.

1. Although Christianity is quite right in believing in the method of starting with the individual, getting him converted, and sending him out to influence the community and change his environment, I feel myself that Christianity should never appear to be content with the present social order. It is bad to concentrate on the individual and leave the social order alone. We must tackle both at the same time, lest the converted man is sent out into a social order that denies those spiritual forces which have brought about his conversion. I am quite sure that the great disparities of wealth common in the world are not according to the mind of God.

2. The challenge comes to us to unite all Christian forces for action. I am sure that very soon, if Christianity is to have the effect in the world which it is capable of having, there must be an end of controversies about orders and sacraments and ritual and ceremonial and denominationalism, and that those who love Christ and believe in his way of life

must unite in their witness and in definite ways of action. I would suggest that the archbishops should call together the leaders of the Free Churches, and together establish good will groups of Christians in every area, in every profession, and in every industry, to seek to show how the mind of Christ could be interpreted most powerfully in the group's particular sphere of activity in the world. The truth is that although Jesus mentioned the kingdom of God about fifty times in the gospel records, we have almost ceased to preach about it at all, and we have done far too little in working out its implications for society. We have been content with an individualistic devotional life, and though there are many splendid Christians about, they are living lives which are largely ineffective in changing the life of the nation. More and more, apart altogether from the group activities just referred to, we must encourage young Christian men and women to take office in the government of their area and subsequently the government of their land. We want more Christian influence where it makes a difference and more Christian voices raised in places where they are listened to and heeded.

3. Lastly, so far as the individual is concerned, we need an inward dedication, an utter self-committal as passionate as that of the communist. We want men and women who will individually say, "As for me, I share Christ's vision of his world-wide kingdom, and I unreservedly commit myself to his cause."

XI

How Should a Christian Regard Sunday?

I CAN TALK ABOUT THIS HIGHLY CONTROVERSIAL SUBJECT ONLY ON THE understanding that I am merely expressing my own point of view. I have no right to suppose that it is any more Christian than that taken by many other people. Please understand, therefore, that I am not saying, "This is right, and that is wrong. This is what you ought to do, and if you do not follow my advice, you are not behaving in a Christian manner." It is an exceedingly important, but a very difficult, subject; and many Christian people—in the name of health and, as they claim, in the name of freedom—would take a very different line from the one I take.

Certainly no man can say to another, "I have all the light there is on this subject." All that one can do is to think aloud, to express the position that one has reached after much discussion with others, much heart searching, and much thought over a long period of time. I think that I ought to warn you in advance that some of my dearest friends think that in regard to this matter of Sunday I am hopelessly old-fashioned and out-of-date.

No one, of course, wants to go back to the attitude to the Sabbath day that was held in the time of our Lord. When we read his liberating words, it is important that we should understand the kind of situation with which he was dealing, for it was very different from our own. For example, some people spend Sunday morning digging their garden. If they had done that in our Lord's day, they would have been stoned to death. Few people today have any conception of the strict laws which protected the Sabbath day when Jesus taught in Palestine. For example, under the general law, "Thou shalt bear no burden on the Sabbath," it was solemnly set down, as a by-law, that while a woman could have a ribbon sewed into her dress, it must not be merely pinned on. If it was merely pinned, it was not secure enough to be regarded as part of her dress, and in wearing the ribbon with a pin she was carrying a burden. Under the same heading it was solemnly set down that false teeth were not to be worn on the Sabbath. That was carrying another burden. Some of the older Jews and Jewesses could not have looked their best on the Sabbath!

Again, you will have noticed that the word "bridge" never occurs in the New Testament, for the simple reason that there were no bridges in Palestine. The only river needing one is the Jordan, and that was forded. In the winter some of the streams would be in flood, but the Jews had a habit of wearing stilts in order to keep dry. They were not, however, allowed to do so on the Sabbath, for the carrying of stilts, with the worthy object of crossing a stream to get to a synagogue, was the carrying of a burden.

We can understand the injunction that reaping was not to be allowed on the Sabbath, but it is ludicrous to read that a woman was not allowed to use a mirror on the Sabbath, for if she did, she might see a gray hair and pull it out, and pulling out gray hairs was reaping.

We can understand the injunction that you must not plow on the Sabbath, but when it is solemnly set down that to drag a stick along the ground, or mark the earth by moving a chair, is plowing, we understand how farcical the law about the Sabbath had become.

Perhaps the most absurd illustration is that which prohibited traveling on the Sabbath. Only a specified limit of two thousand paces was allowed. This was "a Sabbath day's journey." If a man wanted to go beyond that distance, however, he might deposit some trinket, or he could bury a parcel of food, at the end of the two thousand paces, and then, in the eyes of the law, he was justified in regarding that as his temporary dwelling place, since he ate there or kept his goods there. So he could then proceed on another two thousand paces, defeating, of course, by this childish trick the whole purpose of the law.

We can understand the anger of Jesus when his disciples were criticized for pulling a few ears of corn, since he was thoroughly conversant with the means by which the Pharisees themselves eluded the whole purpose of the law in ways that a child could see through. There is rather a lovely saying of Jesus not included in the Gospels but in a document discovered much later, thought to be authentic. Jesus is said to have seen a man working in his garden on the Sabbath day and to have said this illuminating thing to him: "If thou knowest not what thou doest, cursed art thou and a transgressor of the law, but if thou knowest what thou doest, blessed art thou and a true son of Israel." That is a sentence well worth quiet contemplation.

My first point, then, is that before we take the words of our Lord that the Sabbath was made for man and not man for the Sabbath, and excuse the liberties we take with Sunday by reference to that sentence, we ought to have at the back of our minds a picture of the hidebound and absurd system which Jesus was aiming to break. It was a system which pretended to guard the Sabbath for God, but which became a childish and meaningless bundle of irritating and trifling regulations which brought the solemn command of Moses into disrepute. No one ever again, of course, will hedge round the seventh day with regulations like that.

My second point must be a glad readiness to admit that, just as we do not want to go back to the Sabbath of the first century, we do not want to go back to many things connected with the Sunday of the nineteenth century. Some of its restrictions did not make Sunday the glad and happy day it ought to be, but a gloomy day full of prohibitions. Dickens tells us, in *Little Dorrit,* about a man who hated to hear the church bells ring, so unhappy were all the ideas associated with Sunday. And Ruskin said that Monday morning was the happiest time of the week for him —the only person I have ever read about who felt happy on Monday morning—because he said there were at least six days before the dreaded, hated, and miserable Sunday came round again.

Yet over against this I must set my own little bit of evidence. In my childhood I was brought up in a Presbyterian home which, compared with modern standards, would be called very strict. Sunday meant Sunday school twice and chapel twice, with a prayer meeting after the evening service. And if you did not stay to the prayer meeting but went for a walk—and especially if you went for a walk with a person of the opposite sex—well, you felt that in the parental opinion your immortal soul was definitely being threatened! Yet I must also add that the Sundays of my childhood remain in my memory as days of great happiness. Frankly it never occurred to any of us to do anything else on Sunday but attend church and Sunday school. What would have happened if we had suddenly decided to go for a day's picnic, I don't know. Yet Sundays were not irksome and unpleasant, and I do not think there were many homes in which there was more laughter and fun than in mine.

It must not be supposed that those who, in the late 1890's and early 1900's, kept Sunday more strictly than it is kept now were all of them long-faced, gloomy, and miserable.

Now, of course, we live in different times, and Sunday, the keeping of which, I am quite sure, has played an important part in the development of national character, is speedily going. It is really important that we should decide what our attitude is going to be, for I cannot underline too heavily this sentence: *if things go on as they are proceeding now, your grandchildren will have no Sunday left to discuss.* There won't be any difference between Sunday and the other days of the week. Even if you had no interest in Christianity, you might consider asking the question whether, on other grounds, something should not be done to keep one day in seven different from the rest, but in my own view there is a very strong case for guarding the Christian Sunday.

The one parable in this connection which I ask you to try to remember and to discuss round your table is this. Near my home in a London suburb there is a little park. Formerly it was just the grounds of a gentleman's house, and the Borough Council have taken it over and made it into a very pleasant little spot. There are lovely flowerbeds, beautiful lawns, shady trees, a rock garden, and a little pool where two rather tired ducks make the best of the muddy water. Nevertheless, I do not sneer at this little oasis in a London suburb. The action of our Borough Council is to be commended. They have railed round this little park with iron railings, and they lock it at night. There are notices which say, "Please do not pick the flowers," and "Please keep off the grass."

One might say, "Why the palings and the prohibitory notices? Why not leave people free to do what they like?" But I am quite sure that the answer is this: if there were no notices, there would soon be no flowers; and if there were no prohibitions, there would soon be no little park for anybody to enjoy at all. Many people, of course, would respect that little haunt of peace where one may sit on a quiet sunny afternoon and meditate, but many others would not. The Borough Council has even appointed a stalwart guardian who assumes a fiercesome demeanor, especially to little boys who disregard the notices; and as a resident in the borough I would support the appointment of this friend, and I would support the maintenance of the palings and the notices, and they give me just the parable I want.

Sunday is a little park in the noisy din of our hectic week. Sunday is a little oasis in the desert of our monotonous and unnatural life. But I believe that, human nature being what it is, Sunday must be protected and guarded by a number of "Thou shalt nots," or else very soon there will be no Sunday for anybody to enjoy. As I say, if you take no action in this generation, two generations hence there will be nothing to take action about. Sunday will have gone, and those who sneer at some of us and call us narrow-minded old fogies who are trying to hold back the wheels of progress may then ask whether it really was progress, and whether the pace of life has not brought the population, at least of great cities, to the verge of insanity. It is not far from that now.

Mind, it is important to add this at once. If a group of us could go and live together on a desert island, and I had any say in how we were to conduct our life together, I should suggest that on Sunday morning we should have an early morning service, and then rambles through the woods or up into the mountains, and then afternoon tennis matches in full swing and a picnic on the beach, and should wind up the day with a lovely evening service and family prayers at sunset, followed, perhaps, by some good music and good intellectual fellowship concerning the problems of life. You see, on a desert island there would be no outsiders ready to take advantage of our way of spending our day and twist our manner of life to support their desire to paganize Sunday. So on God's day on that desert island we could fulfill his will and find health of body, health of mind, and health of soul.

During World War I, when I was a chaplain serving with troops in the Mesopotamian Desert, that is pretty well the way in which we did spend Sunday, but I emphasize that *we were separated from the rest of society*. If we did that now, the unperceiving all around us who were not in our fellowship would take advantage of our freedom to play games, and they would probably leave out our desire for intellectual health and our determination to give time to worship for the sake of our spiritual health, and, in the name of freedom, they would entirely paganize the whole of the week.

Look, then, at the logical conclusion of what I have said. I am not pretending that there is anything wrong, in the sense of being immoral or wicked, in Sunday games. A game of tennis that is entirely moral on Saturday evening cannot, in itself, be an immoral act on Sunday. Something which keys up the body and keeps it fit is a good thing; and, as I said before, the question is not whether this is right and that is wrong, whether this is good and that is bad, but whether this good thing is making a better thing impossible; whether, in fact, my action on Sunday is contributing to the destruction of Sunday by those who have excluded religion from their list of the most important things of life.

As it seems to me, we have to appear to be more narrow-minded than we really are. We have to seem to condemn Sunday games and motion pictures and the other invasions of Sunday that are coming from all directions, because our apparent censure is the only way of guarding Sunday from those vandals who would destroy it altogether. If you and I walked through the park, in my parable, we should respect the grass edges. We should not pull the flowers, and we should have no need of the iron palings and the gate that is locked at night. In an ideal world, as on a desert island with a chosen community, Sunday games and so on might well have their place, for in an ideal world men would give heed to the needs of their souls as sensibly as they give heed to the needs of their bodies. But until that state of idealism is reached, I think it is important, even at the risk of appearing narrow-minded, to refrain from and, if possible, to prohibit invasions of Sunday just because any other policy destroys a valuable and lovely institution for the whole community.

I would specially ask young Christian people who are in love, for whom marriage is in sight, and those who have just begun their married life together, to think this problem through very carefully. At some point or other your children will ask you what your point of view is and why they are not encouraged to play games on Sunday and so on, and I think when you do discuss the matter together, you should ask yourself this question: Is my attitude to be based on what I may do without being condemned and without my conscience being disturbed, and without being called narrow-minded? Or is my action to be based on what seems to me a far finer basis, namely, What is the finest contribution that I can make to the highest good of the community?

I don't think it is fair for any of us to rebuke someone who plays tennis on Sunday, and say, "You are doing wrong." But in the light of the facts, is he making the best contribution he can to society, or is he consciously doing something which is pulling Sunday down, making the little park into the same kind of jungle as the other days of the week are already? I don't think we should say to the person who goes to the movies or the theater on Sunday, "You are doing wrong." Indeed, before the church can say much about that, she ought to do something far more positive than condemnation. She might well work for the showing of a different type of film on Sundays, for there are lonely towns where there is nothing else to do on a wet night, and I applaud the action of Arthur Rank, who has the moral and spiritual tone of film making very much at heart.

The Christian idealist is not at his best if he condemns others. He is at his best when, at some sacrifice to himself and disregarding the criticisms which may be leveled at him, he makes a positive contribution in the shape of an example which would cleanse and uplift society if it were widely followed.

If this attitude to Sunday games and so on seems narrow-minded, let me state one or two interesting facts. On the day on which the London County Council permitted Sunday games in the parks, the Underground Railway ran one extra train every five minutes. Sportsmen have to be transported. In other words, in order that A may have his Sunday game, B loses his little private park of peace. His Sunday is taken away from him. You may say, "Well, he gets another day instead, and he is quite happy about it." But in the first place there is not any other day that is quite the same—a day on which he could worship if he wants to and a day on which other people are not working either. I can vouch for this because I work on Sunday, and people say, "You can take Monday," but by half past eight Monday morning my telephone is ringing, and by nine o'clock there is something like a hundred letters at the office. No one would ever dream of ringing another up about some ordinary matter early Sunday morning, but no other day has this immunity from the excessive demands that are made upon us.

Further, because another says, "It is all right with me as long as I get paid extra for working on Sunday, or have it made up to me," the question is not thereby solved. For the welfare of the community we have to base our conduct, not on what is agreeable to a person, but on what is good for the whole community. Again you will say to me, "Yes, but your Sunday evening congregation comes by the Underground Railway or by bus, and that involves the work of another." But if the work of another facilitates the worship of God, it is in the same category as my own. The bus driver who brings the congregation to church is, in a sense, a minister of Christ, save that he may not recognize that he is serving the purposes of God. Therefore his activity on Sunday is in quite a different category. It is in the same category as my own work.

Let me turn to another fact. It is the simple fact that Sunday-school and Bible class work cannot be expected to compete with football games and tennis matches. We can imagine a village where an enthusiastic clergyman is doing his utmost to make his Sunday school a success, but on a summer Sunday the village courts are thronged with sportsmen playing tennis. What chance has the minister of getting the best of the boys to his Sunday school? There are a lot of people who sneer at the work of the Sunday school. Indeed, it is used as a derogatory adjective and almost as an epithet, but only by ignorant people. The modern Sunday school, with its clay modeling and sand trays and picture books for the little ones, with its movies and its carefully prepared talk and subsequent discussion for the older ones, is a magnificent contribution to the health of the nation, and in the minds of children religion is being associated with flowers and music and joy, and characters are being steadied and values are being established in children's minds which will have results out of all proportion through all the days of their lives. Many parents of my own generation who were brought up in the Sunday school, but who did nothing in the way of religious teaching for their children, tell me how troubled they are by the indifference to religion of their children now that the latter have reached adolescence. But it is because no anchor was put down in early days and no sense of values was established when the children were young.

When you come to discuss the question of your attitude to Sunday, ask yourself which is the greater contribution to the life of the nation: the religious work of the Sunday school or the physical exercise of the tennis match, remembering that the old, whining complaint that people have no time except on Sundays to enjoy themselves is canting hypocrisy. Most of you have every Saturday and Sunday free and every evening of the week as well, and on summer evenings it is light for a long time.

Here is a third fact which seems to me of great importance. If you study the crime reports, you will hardly ever find a young person in the courts who has, for any length of time, attended a Sunday school or Bible class. That is a fact. If, in the name of liberty or health, you are going to argue that young people should turn to sport on Sunday, then you are going to kill the Sunday school, and you must make up your mind which of those two you think is the more worthy of survival.

I expect you would laugh at me if I put the picture of my old home against the modern picture of a home today. Yet I can scarcely help doing it. We youngsters set off for morning Sunday school and went on to the church service, came back to dinner and, as soon as we were old enough, discussed the sermon! After dinner we went back to Sunday school. My father and mother both taught in it. Some lonely person who had only lodgings to go to would be brought back for tea, and we all went to the evening service. After the evening service on Sundays my home would fill up with lonely folk whom my mother or father would invite along to supper. We were not rich, but we shared what we had, and there was plenty of laughter and plenty of willing hands to lighten the extra housework involved. And then at about ten o'clock there would be family prayers and two or three hymns round the piano. You may sneer, if you like, or feel sorry for me, but it was a very happy day, and there was a peace and joy and serenity about it that has meant much to me. Frankly, I haven't found these lovely assets in many homes since.

I cannot feel that that is a poorer way of spending Sunday than the modern one in which father potters about in the garden on Sunday morning, or stays in bed, or goes to golf, and John goes off on his motor bike to some unknown destination, from which he returns at midnight, and Mary goes off with some friends to play tennis and on to a cocktail party. Nobody knows where anybody else is. Home is only a convenient place in which to take meals more cheaply than in a restaurant and, last thing at night, a useful place to sleep more cheaply than in a hotel. You will accuse me of painting the picture with less love in it than there actually is. But frankly I am troubled about modern home life. It does not seem to me to contain the stabilizing, morale-producing element that it used to possess. We make our cheap sneers at the Puritans and imagine that they were long-faced and melancholy spoilsports. Many things they thought important I am glad we have outgrown, but I wish we had their stability of character, their sense of obligation, their self-discipline, and, perhaps above all, their sense that it was worth while to serve the community without always thinking of benefit for oneself. At any rate, I think the Puritans made a greater contribution to the life of their time than is being made by some of the superficial young people of our own day, who criticize others most violently, but who seem concerned only to squeeze as much pleasure as they can out of life, who never think sacrificially of the needs of other people, or of service to the community, and who, in a whirl of meaningless inanities, giggle away their days. So many seem to pose in an attempt to be thought the kind of person admired by their own set. They do not seem to be real persons at all.

May I ask you some very rude questions, but will you in your own heart answer them? When did you last do anything for anybody else, for which you were not paid either in money, or prestige, or popularity? When, outside your own family and the circle of your own immediate pals, did you do anything for anybody else? When did you last give up doing something on which you had set your heart, in order to help another? Living your life, as you do, in the little circle of your own friends and in the round of pleasures which every week you map out for yourself, have you ever stopped to think how many people there are who have fallen stricken by the wayside, how many lonely folk there are, how many broken hearts there are, how many invalids there are whom no one ever visits and children for whom no one ever cares? Do you realize just how much unhappiness and frustration and misery there is, and do you realize the enormous dividend that comes to the one who invests even an hour a week in unselfish service? Don't excuse yourself by saying, "Well, I don't know how to set about helping others." There is a Samaritan League here at the City Temple for men. There is a League of Service for women. There are a thousand organizations in London in which you could show your sincerity. And when you say, "Yes, but I haven't the time," you will forgive me for saying you have every Sunday, and you must decide whether on that day you are *always* going to plan for *your* fun, *your* pleasure, *your* happiness, or whether on God's day you might engage in God's service.

Everybody is eloquent about the things that are wrong and is ready to grumble at the imposed austerities of these days. What about spending one hour each week helping to put things right in any one of the thousand ways open to you? What about leaving the sideline of life, from the safety of which it is so easy to criticize the players, and for an hour a week playing on a team?

I would make one further appeal for Sunday on the grounds on which Moses made it. No one believes today that Moses went up into a mountain with a slab of stone and came down with words written on it by the actual finger of God. Certainly the biblical writer never intended such a crude interpretation to be put on the poetry of his message. But when Moses, that great, unselfish leader of his community, thought out the rules which would keep his people healthy and good, he borrowed from an older code, the Code of Hammurabi (2100 B.C.), which contained an old Babylonian law that on the seventh day men should rest. Indeed, the Babylonian word for "Sabbath" is a picturesque word meaning "stop" or "halt." Stop doing what you are doing! Push away all these hectic activities of every day! Stop forever trying to make money, and be quiet! Let us remember that the word "holy" and the word "whole" and the word "healthy" all come from the same root. You could even translate the commandment about the Sabbath to read: "Remember the Sabbath Day to keep it healthy," health for the body, health for the mind, and health for the spirit. To do all three every Sunday may be asking a lot, but I think that is the ideal to aim at, as long as we can do it without behaving in a way which can be used or misused to deprive others of the privilege we wish for ourselves.

Many say that the wealthy man can privately play tennis on his own court, and why should not the poor man be allowed to do it also? But what private people do cannot so easily be legislated for. If we decide that something a person privately does is not to be encouraged, it is strange logic to argue that, *because* he does it, public money shall be spent on making it easy for the poor to follow him.

"Why can't we all do what we like?" someone says. "Why should religious people constrain others? Pagans don't prohibit them from going to their churches. Why should the churchgoer prohibit the pagan his games?" But if religious people have a vision of what is best for the community, they must not only be examples of their principles, but propagate them as enthusiastically as they can. It is a strange logic that says, "Let us all do what we like." To my mind the man who cares nothing for Sunday is a menace to the community; and, by exerting his freedom, he is plotting the captivity of all in what will become increasingly a Sunday-less week.

Do realize how insidiously and quickly men take advantage and misuse what they call liberty. If the community says to one man, "Certainly, you can play tennis," what right has it to say to another man, "You may not open your shop on Sunday and make a little more money to tide over a difficult time of illness"? When the community says, "Yes, we will have great football games on Sunday," it will very quickly say to the restaurants, "Yes, certainly the sportsmen have to be fed."

So we come to the last argument of the Sunday-breaker. Did not Jesus say that "the sabbath was made for man, and not man for the sabbath"? Yes, he did. And what is man? If man is only a mixture of iron and carbon and phosphorus and water and so on, don't let us bother about Sunday. If man, as someone has said, is "an animal on his way to the dung heap"; if he is only a machine that grinds out wages and passes quickly into nothingness, well, don't let us bother. But if man is a living spirit, if the life of his soul depends on his communion with the divine, what then? When Jesus said, "The sabbath was made for man, and not man for the sabbath," he added, "Therefore the Son of man is Lord also of the sabbath."

Let me finish with one picture. A little while ago I was called to see an old man who was dying, and who was very frightened of death, as some people are. And when, as tenderly as I could, I tried to talk to him about God and religion and the soul, he said, very bitterly and brokenly, mumbling as he said the words, "I have led a very busy life. I have never had time for that sort of thing." *But he had had four thousand Sundays!*

XII

Is Every Christian a Priest?

Ye also, as lively stones, are built up . . . an holy priesthood, to offer up spiritual sacrifices, acceptable to God by Jesus Christ. —I Pet. 2:5

[*He*] *hath made us . . . priests unto God and his Father.* —Rev. 1:6

LISTEN FIRST TO SOME WORDS OF JOHN GICHTEL:

If I bear my sinful brother, as Christ took our sin upon Himself, and ever confess his misery as my own, and pray for mercy and grace, that God in Christ may look down upon me and help me to bear and subdue my brother's sin and give me his soul, then I am a priest of God. This royal priesthood is a very deep mystery, and those who bear this office are pupils under God's immediate eye, and His beloved children, who enter into the Holiest of Holies. They enter the strife for their brethren and help them by prayer and by the offering up of their life for them that they also may overcome. The soul that is anointed for the priesthood of God must thus fill up what remains of the sufferings of Christ.

The question is, What is a priest? One dictionary I consulted said that a priest is "one who has authority to administer the sacrament and pronounce absolution." I accept the definition, but the doctrine I want to expound is that of the priesthood of *all* believers.

In John's Gospel, chapter twenty, verse twenty-three, it is recorded that Jesus said to those gathered in the upper room, "Whose soever sins ye remit, they are remitted unto them; and whose soever sins ye retain, they are retained." The Roman Catholic Church has taken that passage as its authority for declaring that a priest, in the Roman Catholic sense, alone can grant absolution. The exaggerated claims which Roman Catholics make in this connection can be seen from two quotations. Here is the first from Father Hunter's book called *Dogmatic Theology:*

The priest's absolution is not merely a pronouncement that a penitent has been forgiven; it is "a judicial act," and the word of absolution is *per se* efficacious, even though spoken "not seriously but in joke." Its efficacy does not depend on the character of the priest: even "priests who are in mortal sin have power to bind and loose." The reason is that it is the rite of ordination that confers the authority of absolution. And it follows that only a priest possesses that authority: "priests alone can give absolution." [1]

Similarly, the Tridentine fathers declared that Christ "before he ascended into heaven . . . granted that power to bishops and presbyters in the church," and that "mortal sin does not incapacitate them for the office." Rome does not allow that sacerdotal absolution is simply a declaration that the penitent is pardoned. It is a real bestowal upon him of the divine pardon itself.[2]

The Encyclical of Pope Pius X, February 11, 1906, declares:

The Church is the mystical Body of Christ, a Body ruled by Pastors and Teachers, a society of men headed by rulers having full and perfect powers of governing, instructing and judging. It follows that this Church is essentially an unequal society, that is to say, a society comprising two categories of persons; pastors and the flock, those who hold rank in the different degrees of the hierarchy and the multitude of the faithful. And these categories are so distinct in themselves that in the pastoral body alone reside the necessary right and authority to guide and direct all the members towards the goal of the society. As for the multitude, it has no other right than that of allowing itself to be led and, as a docile flock, to follow its shepherds.

We see at once how much depends on the answer to the question, Who were the people gathered in the upper room to whom Jesus spoke these tremendous words? Were they the eleven alone? Assuredly not. There is not a shred of support here for the Roman Catholic claim that the priest alone can forgive or retain sin, let alone the outrageous claim that even if he is joking, or if he is in a state of mortal sin himself, he can forgive others just because he is a priest.

Let us notice very carefully that the phrase "the disciples" has both a general and a particular use in the New Testament. I have the authority of a first-rate New Testament scholar, Professor J. Alexander Findlay, [3]

[1] P. 776.
[2] This is from the late Professor C. J. Cadoux's volume, *Catholicism and Christianity*, p. 414.
[3] In a personal letter to me.

for saying that while in Mark and Matthew the "disciples" are the twelve, in John, where occurs the passage in question, they are called "the twelve," and the phrase "the disciples" means *"a wider circle of less closely attached followers."* [4] Dr. Cadoux, of Mansfield College, Oxford, agrees, and in a letter to me writes, "I agree with you that it would be impossible to prove that these [the people addressed by Jesus on the night of Easter Day] were only the eleven."

We get light on our problem by turning to Luke's parallel passage of the words spoken by Jesus to his followers on the night of the Resurrection.[5] Here we find that those gathered in the upper room are described as "the eleven gathered together, *and them that were with them,"* a company which seems to have included women.[6] It is therefore of immense importance to realize that the authority to declare, with conviction, that another is forgiven, or that his sins are retained, was not an authority given only to priests or to ministers, *but to all followers of Christ.*

As Dean Inge said in a newspaper article, "The Christian Church was founded by laymen for laymen. This is an indisputable fact. It was prophetic and unsacerdotal from the first. Our Lord placed himself in the prophetic succession; he was known as the prophet from Galilee. And the prophets were not priests. The twelve apostles were all laymen; there was no priest among them. Paul was a layman." My friend the Rev. Henry T. Wigley commenting on this says, "Dr. Inge is right in maintaining that in the Early Church there was no sacerdotalism and no radical difference as between clergy and laity, but to be more in keeping with the New Testament we would prefer to say that in the Early Church there were no laymen, for all were priests." [7]

In other words, the Anglican and Free Church view of the priesthood is sound, and it is important that we should expound it to the people. The priest is not essentially different from any other disciples; and when it is said that the disciples may remit or retain sin, what is being said is that the disciples, by virtue of the spiritual insight of discipleship, can decide whether a person is sincere or not, and thus whether he is forgiven or not, and can declare the endless forgiveness of God. Having this

[4] See John 4:1; 6:66-67; 7:3; 18:25; 19:38; and so forth.
[5] Luke 24:33-43.
[6] See vss. 10, 22-24.
[7] In the *Free Church Chronicle*, July, 1947.

insight, they must show the charity of those who do not identify the sinner with his sin, and who therefore help him to break away from it, by believing him capable of being rid of it through the grace of Christ which they themselves have experienced. It is that experience of having been forgiven himself that gives the disciple authority to declare the forgiveness of God to others. How often we have "retained" the sin of men and driven them to despair through our cynicism or contempt, through our hardness or disapproval, when a warm belief in the splendid possibilities of those who sin would have helped the sinner to be rid of his sin. We are ready enough in our own case to separate the thought of ourselves from the sins which we commit. We say, "I wasn't myself that day." But we are not always ready to do that with others. When they have let us down, we are inclined to condemn them forever and even to hold them in contempt, identifying them with the things they do. By this unchristian attitude we "retain" their sins. The Greek word "to retain" means "to cause to stick to a person." The Greek word for "remit" means "to leave behind." And it is important to spend a little time on those two words "remit" and "retain" in order to make clear to ourselves that Jesus is not conferring a priestly rite on a small group of his followers, but telling all those who love him and follow him that they must be ready to declare the forgiveness of God to the sinner—a fact that does not even wait on the sinner's penitence [8]—and then in all personal relationships to treat that sinner as a forgiven person, lest, identifying him permanently with his sins, we make them stick to him, depriving ourselves of the possibility of seeing the sinner as a forgiven person freed from his sin and holding down the sinner—because of our disbelief in him—in the depressing shackles of his own faults.

Any person who has been forgiven by Christ has Christ's authority to pronounce absolution to another, for all Christ's disciples are his priests.

Lest it should seem that in this most important matter of the priesthood of all believers I am putting forward an interpretation of my own, let me give you three quotations from unimpeachable authorities.

Martin Luther claimed that any Christian—even a woman or child—could do for one what the priest does in this matter, and in his great book

[8] Cf. Jesus' prayer for those who crucified him: "Father, forgive them." By making forgiveness wait on penitence we reduce the free grace of God to a pagan bargain. Penitence is not the condition of God's forgiving, but of the sinner's *receiving* forgiveness.

already quoted Professor Cadoux shows how the Pope in 1520 condemned Luther for this claim.[9]

My second quotation is from no less a scholar than Westcott, who, in his *Commentary on the Gospel of St. John,* says:

> There is nothing to show that the gift [of remitting and retaining sin] was confined to any particular group such as the apostles among the whole company present. The commission, therefore, must be regarded properly as the commission of the Christian society and not that of the Christian ministry.[10]

My third quotation is from the late Archbishop of Canterbury, Dr. Temple:

> The authority here bestowed is given to the body of Christians, not, or at least not necessarily or certainly, to any one member of that body. . . . To the Church, as the fellowship of the Spirit, is given the authority of Christ Himself as Pardoner and Judge. But only so far as the Church in and through its members fulfils the condition—Receive the Holy Spirit—can it discharge this function.[11]

The Free Churches have always emphasized this doctrine of the priesthood of all believers. They do not regard the ordained minister as essentially different from any other disciple of Christ. It is *convenient* that one person should be given a training in special subjects, and it is *convenient* that he should be set aside from the ordinary, secular toil of the world and given opportunities for prayer and study. He should have a careful training in the science of the human mind in order that, dealing with troubled people every day, he may be a more useful instrument in the hands of God. But it is only a matter of convenience, just as one member of the directorate in a firm may be trained and set aside to deal with one particular aspect of the firm's business, or just as one member of the community is trained as a policeman and given special authority to act for the community in certain ways. The minister has not received in himself, by the laying on of the hands of some ecclesiastical superior, anything different from that which is available to every disciple.

I was ordained by the laying on of hands. Such a solemn service, with attendant ritual, is bound to be an occasion of the reception of grace,

[9] Pp. 413-14.
[10] P. 295.
[11] *Readings in St. John's Gospel,* II, 387.

but the act of laying on of hands does not mechanically provide a channel for grace. In brutal language, nothing passes from the ordaining hands which was not the possession of the ordinand before. Unless the ordinand had his "orders" from Christ, he has no right to be ordained. And the person who carries out the service of ordination—a service rich in grace to the ordinand and all present—does not *mechanically* convey grace. He acknowledges something that Christ has done in the soul of the ordinand and something the church has done in training him; and, accepting that, the ordaining person, whether bishop or minister, formally gives the ordinand the authority of the church to act in certain ways as one of the church's representatives.

The idea that grace can be mechanically conveyed by the laying on of hands is to me a medieval superstition. Surely "orders" can come only from God, and I think they come from God via the people who are going to receive the ministrations of the ordinand. I think the ordinand—who should be in his study by the time other people are at work—should look upon his setting aside as a kind of bargain. If his people are trustful and good enough to say to him, "You may be excused the secular toil which takes so much of our strength, and you may receive a salary which will keep you from want," then he should on his side say, "And I will keep my part of the bargain. During the week I will find time for thought and prayer and study, as well as time to help you in your time of trouble, and I will climb the hilltops, so that when you turn up on Sunday, after a heavy week of work, I shall have news from God to tell you and to keep your faith burning during your life on the plains." I myself cannot accept the idea that a priest is essentially different from any other disciple, and I would as soon take the Holy Communion from the hands of a saintly lady, or a devoted charwoman, or a dedicated carpenter, as from the hands of a bishop, or archbishop, or Free Church ecclesiastical superior. Nor can I believe that there would be any hindrance to the grace that would come to me if I thus received the holy symbols.

I am afraid I have spent much time in opening up the subject in this way, but it seems necessary to do so in order that I may define what I mean by a priest. I should not accept the dictionary definition in that exclusive form, but rather define a priest thus: a priest is a representative of the Christian fellowship who continually goes to God for men and to men for God. Hold that definition in mind. Ponder it, and see if you agree with it. A priest is for convenience set apart and trained, but he is only a representative of the whole number of the disciples, and you, because you are a follower of Christ, are a priest. Every time you say, "Our Father," you bring in the rest of the world, and in every prayer of intercession you are going to God for men. Then, when you go back to your work, just because you are a Christian disciple your work is not merely a convenient way of earning a living. You are going to men for God. You are offering your job as a contribution to the coming of his kingdom, and unless that job is in itself evil, it can be offered to God just as much as the work of the holy ministry. Indeed, I can do my work with the wrong motive of trying to get glory for myself out of it, and a woman can scrub a kitchen, as George Herbert pointed out, with the motive of making that work more truly divine than the chanting of psalms. The woman who cleans the house, gets the meals, manages with insufficient help, and who at the same time can keep radiant and cheerful and happy so that, as the poem says, "She lights the kitchen with God's love" as she prepares the bread and wine of life, is just as much a priest as the one who lifts the bread and wine from the holy table and offers it to the people of God.

I feel that one of the great lessons of the Reformation is often neglected. The very architecture of St. Sepulchre's Church in London is an illustration of what I mean. Behind the pulpit, from which John Wesley preached more than once, you can see high up in the north wall the mark of a door, through which the priest came from the monastery to read the Bible to the people—for few could read—and then to join the other clergy behind the screen which ran right across the church. The clergy were on one side of the screen, the laity on the other. In some churches you may still see the screen in this position. The clergy were removed from the life of the world, and were not to be diverted from their vows by even gazing upon the laity. There was, indeed, a division between the sacred and the secular.

But now the only screen is behind the back pew. It is useful to keep out the draft and the sounds of the street; but if I may press the illustration, we may say that the screen is behind the last member to enter the church. And that does not mean that the whole gathering has become secular. It means that the whole community have become priests.

This doctrine of the priesthood of all believers is far-reaching in two ways, and very important for our modern life, for one of the great dangers of today is that religion tends to be withdrawn from the life of the community and irrelevant to the daily tasks of men.

1. We must say more and more to people, "You are not to think of your task as secular and unrelated to religion. You are to be as a priest who offers all his service to God." We all remember the story of the juggler turned monk, who one night was found doing his juggling tricks before the high altar. If I remember the story rightly, he was praised for doing this. He was offering God that which he could do well. And when we have a little more sense, we shall not ordain people only to the ministry, but to every other trade and profession which Christian men can take up honorably in the life of the world, for all is, or can be, the service of God.

It is easy to see this in some professions like those of the doctor or nurse or teacher, but a little thought will make every job, not in itself evil, shine with the divine light. If work is service to the community, it can rightly be thought of as service to God. In one of my notebooks I have a note of an epitaph written on the tombstone in a village churchyard, which went something like this: "In memory of Thomas Cobb, who mended shoes to the glory of God in this village for forty years." Isn't that grand? For, of course, when Thomas Cobb mended shoes, he did not put in brown paper, but good leather, and knew that he was co-operating with God in answering the prayers of men and women for health in wet weather. How grand it would be to have an ordained charwoman who always came at eight-thirty, and an ordained plumber who did not leave his tools at home and spend half the morning fetching them, an ordained gardener who worked full time whether we were there to watch him or not! And so on. It is all very well to call church worship "divine service," but actually divine service begins with our work on Monday morning.

Dr. George MacLeod, the minister of the Iona Community, with a band of helpers is rebuilding the ancient abbey of St. Colomba, and for three months in the summer ministers and masons and carpenters and plumbers and builders become one community, living under almost monastic conditions, rejoicing in a common fellowship and offering all their work to God. Gradually we shall have not just chaplains to the troops in wartime, but more and more chaplains in factories, for the whole of industry must be redeemed from the realm of the secular and lifted up to God. When we begin to act thus, we shall have a new motive for altering evil things, and we shall be less able to regard our fellows as cogs in a machine, a machine which often grinds down human nature for the benefit of the few. No industry is healthy if any human personality is a means to another person's end. If service to the community is the end, and all men co-operate happily to bring that end about, then such a piece of work can be offered to God, for we can truly serve God only as we serve our fellows.

I hear socialists say on the one hand, "Why don't you drop all this mystical stuff and take up the cause of the working man?" And I hear Christians say on the other hand, "Don't worry about the social order. Convert the working man." I realize with dismay that they are both wrong. The church is left irrelevant to work, and work is separated from the divine blessing. Of course we must worry about the social order. We cannot send even the converted man out into a social order calculated to deny all his new-found ideals, an order which regards him as part of a soulless machine. But we cannot drop all this "mystical stuff," for in God's plan work and worship go together. All men are to be a fellowship of priests offering their daily life and work to the High God.

2. The second way in which this doctrine of the priesthood of all believers is significant is that within our churches—for we must make a start there—there must be a far greater concern for the sufferings and spiritual welfare of others. A young minister recently wrote, telling me of his concern and worry because he had to go to see a dying man. "I hardly know what to say," he wrote. "I am afraid of saying the wrong thing, and it is so very important to say the right thing, or to know if one should say nothing at all." I felt in that letter how true a priest this young minister was. He was bearing the burden of the dying man to whom he was called upon to minister. I am not belittling the value of our training in the ministry to help us cope with our problems, but I think that within a church, at any rate, wherever there is a person whom life has bruised or wounded, we should *all* have the feeling "That is my burden." And every church member should feel held up by recalling that his fellow members do think thus, for truly if we are a fellowship of priests, the burden of one is the burden of all, the wound of one is the wound of all, the trouble of one is the concern of all. Even in religion there is far too much of this selfish Christianity which merely seeks from a service help for the individual's problems. "Let me go to church and see if I can get a bit of help for

myself. Let me read the Bible or this good book, or say my prayers, to get spiritual benefit for myself." Yes, but you would find far greater help and strength rushing into your own life if you made room for God in your own soul by pouring out love upon another stricken by the way.

I want to make the living fellowship which we call the City Temple a priesthood of believers. Note, of *believers,* not mere assenters. I want it to be a fellowship of loving, caring, praying people, who are ready even to suffer that they may serve others, ready even to identify themselves with the troubles of others if those who are wounded by the wayside may be lifted back into the life of communion with God. So we may go to men for God and go to God for men, bring God's love down to those whose lives touch ours, and lift our work up that it may be offered as a sacrifice to the Most High. "[He] hath made us . . . priests unto God and his Father." May we be "built up . . . a holy priesthood, to offer up spiritual sacrifices, acceptable to God by Jesus Christ."

XIII

What Is God's Plan for the Family?

EVERYONE WHO HAS ANY CONCERN AT ALL ABOUT THE WELFARE OF Britain is troubled to note the signs of the disintegration of her family life. The concern of the B.B.C. has been evident in the nature of many recent broadcasts. The Congregational Union sent out a letter recently, over the signature of the president and secretary, inviting all churches to take some step to bring the matter before the people. The letter contained this sentence: "The best traditions of the home are threatened by grave dangers, and the churches of all denominations are called to grapple with an issue that goes down to the roots of our national life."

Even before the war began there were signs that all was not well with the home. Even then no poet could have written the kind of thing that we find in Burns's "The Cotter's Saturday Night":

> The chearfu' supper done, wi' serious face,
> They, round the ingle, form a circle wide;
> The sire turns o'er, wi' patriarchal grace,
> The big ha'-Bible, ance his father's pride.
> His bonnet rev'rently is laid aside. . . .
> . . . .
> He wales a portion with judicious care,
> And "Let us worship God!" he says, with solemn air.

There is probably not one home in the British Isles of which the words of Burns paint a true picture. It is an immense problem, and to deal with it completely would require a book, for I should have to speak of marriage problems, of many sex problems, of the training of children, of the development of adolescents, of the basis of the family unity. But perhaps even in this limited space I can touch on some of the more pressing aspects of this great problem.

First of all I would awaken you, if you need awakening, to the gravity of the situation. It is true that the disintegration of home life began before the war, but the war years immeasurably complicated the situation. Our boys and girls were taken out of the atmosphere of the home and put down in strange places. Some of them suffered very much from loneliness, but others suffered far more from an environment which was highly dangerous to their developing natures. Just when they were beginning to open out in an atmosphere that at any rate *contained* Christian influences, they were transferred to an atmosphere which in many cases was coarse, materialistic, selfish, and even sensual.

Again, many of them made unwise links with the opposite sex. War engagements and war weddings took place between people who never had a chance to get to know one another under normal conditions and for a sufficient length of time. But worse still, without the solemn obligation of an engagement or a wedding, emotional attachments took place and often sex intimacy occurred between young people who did not even intend to begin a home together. The average morality—or perhaps one ought to say immorality—which is characteristic of the age has been one of the most disintegrating features in the life of our people. Further, young people who had begun their home life together and perhaps had one or two children before the war began, were separated for many years. That separation did nothing to strengthen and purify the family life of our country. In many and many a home, health and happiness reigned before the war, but the husband away on service made emotional contacts with other women, or a wife remaining at home had an unhealthy liaison with another man, or both, so that in thousands of homes, on one side or the other, there was unfaithfulness of mind, and often of body, and the renewal of a family life has been beset by fearful difficulties set up by subterfuge, deceit, suspicion, and misunderstanding. Quarrels have followed, and every psychologist knows that quarreling parents mean neurotic children who are inevitably thrust into conflict. The disharmony between their parents divides their loyalty and takes away their sense of security.

It was inevitable, of course, that these years of separation should effect a change in the character and the personality of those who were separated. No one could suppose that two people, even if they really loved one another, could be apart for such a long period and take up their lives again at the point where they left off. Personality is not a static thing. It is constantly developing and growing, and a completely different environment made the change in personality even greater. Even where nothing happened of which either party need be ashamed, and even where two married folk love one another deeply, they should not try to live together again supposing that nothing has altered. If possible, they would be very wise to have another honeymoon and to make every allowance for one another for a year or two, so that a new and happy adjustment can be effected.

In such a situation as I have roughly outlined it is not surprising that many marriages have been wrecked. The Marriage Guidance Council in June of 1945 reported that 10 per cent of modern marriages finished in the divorce court, and the figure would be nearer 20 per cent if it included cases of separation. If one out of ten finishes in the divorce court and two out of ten in separation, how many others are carried on only for the sake of convention or appearance, or for the laudable motive of refraining from breaking the lives of the children born of the marriage? How many carry on in that awful tension of toleration, in a home where love is dead and even friendship difficult? I fear that we must be awake to the fact that in the home life of the nation things are about as bad as they have ever been in our long history. Fourteen thousand couples were divorced in England and Wales in 1944. Think what that means for home life. God's plan is that every child shall have a good father and a good mother. If either goes, the child's sense of security is undermined and his nervous health threatened. Further, one more example of the danger of getting married is held up before the world. A family should be an intimate group of people living together in an atmosphere of good will and good humor, where the joys and successes of one give joy to all, where the troubles and problems and failures of one are the concern of all, where each seeks the welfare of all and all of each.

Having noted that, let us turn back and notice the contrast of modern days with those which form the background of the Old Testament lesson in Josh. 7:16-26. In Old Testament days the family was the basic unit of society and realized as such. The individual had no rights whatever apart from the family. In a sense it was hardly recognized that he existed apart from the family. It was the family which gave to individuals any significance they possessed. It is difficult for us now to realize how the family emphasis dominated the thoughts of men. When we do realize this, we can understand those strange Old Testament stories in which a whole family was put to death for the sin of one. There was no sense of injustice among the Hebrew people in regard, for instance, to the punishment meted out to Achan. He stole, and the whole family was put to death. Nobody felt it unjust. They were all one, and what one did they all did. It is even probably true that some of the Old Testament stories which we loved in childhood and which seem to center about a famous name, like Abraham or Isaac or Jacob, were not stories of an individual, but stories of a tribe. For hundreds of years there was no such thing as individualism in our sense at all.

The Ten Commandments are probably based on the Code of Hammurabi, which dates back as far the other side of the birth of Christ as we are on this side, and we find the same ideas running back to that remote time. According to this code if a builder built a house and it collapsed through bad workmanship, the purchaser had every right to put the builder and every member of his family to death. Many of us have wondered at that old law that said, "The sins of the fathers shall be visited upon the children unto the third and fourth generations." This has sometimes been supposed to be an early reference to the laws of heredity, but we are far too early in history for such an interpretation to be possible. Ideas of inherited consequences had not emerged in human thought. The reference is to the solidity of the family. Great-grandfather, grandfather, father, sons, and grandsons were all involved in the action of any member of the whole clan. The family was a unity. Individualism did not exist.

It is interesting to read that the same situation still holds in China. I read that if a father commits a crime, even in modern China, and the police cannot lay hands on the criminal, they put the rest of the family in jail; and if the father has committed a crime punishable with the capital sentence, his son may be put to death. I quote this to show that individualism is a comparatively late development in human thought.

Now see how human ideas have swung in the West to the opposite extreme. So far from the ancient way of thinking, the family now counts for very little. The individual within the family, let alone within the wider clan involving other generations, asserts his or her rights, often in defiance of anything the family may think and say, and this individualism has become so extreme as to be unhealthy. For thousands of young people in their late teens and early twenties home is merely a useful place to eat and sleep. That is all. These young people are individualists in their pleasure and individualists in their suffering. Their inner mind is often known to no one but themselves. Their rights are individual rights, their problems individual problems, their responsibility individual responsibility. It is cheaper to have one's meals at home than in a restaurant and more convenient to sleep at home, but home is only a restaurant or a dormitory. It is not the center of communal life where the interests of one are the interests of all, where the joys of one are gladly shared by all, and where the troubles of one are cheerfully regarded as the burdens of all. In modern life individualism has gone mad.

When we ask the reasons for this, it is true, no doubt, that ideas of liberty and freedom from the old-time tyranny of parents are partly responsible, but I think an unrealized reason is the awful mechanization in industry. Among all the people you know who set off after breakfast to do their day's work, how many are really able to live as individuals and act as real persons? I think you would find, as you think about them, that most of them are machines. They are complicated, highly organized machines, but machines. They are means to somebody else's ends. The area of life in which a human being can act and live as a real person, as a free individual, has diminished until most ordinary people are imprisoned in an industrial machine from which they cannot escape, in which they are simply cogs in a wheel.

It is not, therefore, surprising to find that when a glorious thing like a human personality is artificially imprisoned in industry and made machine-like, it will find compensation by exaggerated freedom in other directions. If a man cannot escape from the prison of mechanized industry and act as a free person there—and he cannot, because if he did he would lose his job—he will break out of the prison from which he *can* escape without such dire consequences. Therefore he breaks from the restraint of the home, saying, as it were, to himself, "If I am tyrannized over in my daily work and cannot escape, I will not have any unnecessary restraints." His family life suffers. Not only does he claim the right to act only as an individual, but unless he feels the responsibility of fatherhood, he does not feel it necessary even to be loyal to the family. And home is just a cheap lodging.

This is a very serious situation, because family life is still the real basic unit of the life of the nation, and on healthy family life depends the moral and spiritual health of the nation. Students will remember that, in the opinion of Gibbon, what brought Rome down into that frightful debacle was not the opposition of the enemy without the gate, but the disintegration of family life within the home. Home life in ancient Rome frequently descended into orgies of sexuality and license in which the true values perished. If once the home life of this country disintegrates, it will not be long before her national supremacy is lost and our beloved country becomes a third-, fourth-, or fifth-class power, or even sinks into that limbo of forgotten civilizations which God can no longer use. It must have been hard for Romans, in the heyday of Rome's might, to think that disaster could ever happen to Rome. It is hard to think that we could so fall, but the relentless lesson of history cannot be escaped, and we have to say to ourselves that the threat to our nation from within its home life is far greater than the threat of Germany ever was to our truest interests.

I think I can best use the space that remains by talking to the young people, many of whom have not yet begun to set up their home life together. I trust, indeed, that some things said already may help to put things right for those whose home life is undermined and threatened. I even hope to help some whose home life has fallen in ruins around them through some of the causes outlined earlier. But at any rate I will now speak to those who really want to establish a truly Christian home. In doing so they can probably serve the nation more truly than in any other way open to them.

1. First of all, then, decide in some quiet hour what the values are that you are determined to preserve in your home. For instance, do you really believe in God, and do you think he should count in your home life? What will be your attitude to Sunday? Is religion to be a subject about which you are shy and embarrassed, or even a little ashamed, or is it to be something about which you are quite open and frank? Is it to be an unashamedly religious home in the best sense of the word—not goody-goody and narrow-minded and intolerant of others' views, but lit up by the healthy religion associated with that young Man who stood upon the shore of Galilee so long ago and said those things which have changed the history of the world? Do you think truth and beauty and kindness and loyalty and frankness are values that should be guarded? A lady I interviewed a short time ago said, among many other things, "We never say what we really think in our family. I suppose they don't in any family." I wish she could stay with me! They tell you the truth in my family! As you set up your home, why not decide to put away all artificiality and insincerity? Why, in so many homes, does everybody

hide behind defense mechanisms, never daring to be himself or herself, always taking refuge in disguise and pose and pretense? At home we should be mentally relaxed and most truly ourselves. No one should be allowed to be pompous, dominating, and self-important. No, not even father! There should be for all an atmosphere of reality, confidence, security, healthy sympathy, and good will. No one should be afraid of anyone, or make selfish or unreasonable demands of another. We should give and take, consider others, speak and act freely, and dissolve irritation in the reagent of fun.

2. Having decided on values, decide on the means by which you intend to retain those values. May I mention four important points under this heading?

a) What about family prayers until the little people get into their teens or go away to boarding school? If you say, "Well, that's old-fashioned and out of date," I reply, "It's a pity to let a good habit like that get out of date." Dr. Paton, missionary to the Hebrides, used to crouch outside his father's bedroom door to hear him pray. He wrote:

> If everything else in religion were by some accident blotted out, my soul would go back to those days of reality. For sixty years my father kept up the practice of family prayer. None of us can remember that any day passed without it. No hurry for business or market, no arrival of friends or guests, no trouble or sorrow, no joy or excitement, ever prevented us from kneeling round the family altar while our high priest offered himself and his children to God.

Paton's father was a farm laborer.

If you say, "Well, we haven't time," I just don't believe it. There is a splendid book published by the Student Christian Movement called *Two-Minute Bible Readings*. There are scores of books of prayers printed. Everybody could finish the breakfast meal with a three-minute turning to God. I am not pressing for this when children have grown up or gone to boarding school where this matter is taken care of, but one of the ways of showing that God matters in your home is to have a family recognition of God at least once a day, until the thought of God and the importance of religion are established in the mind of every member.

Forgive me if I put on record my own very unimportant witness. My father and mother were always very busy. I cannot remember that we had help in the home until I was grown up. But I cannot remember one morning—however busy they were, and however excited we might be at forthcoming holidays, and so on—when family prayers were forgotten, until we reached the teens. In a meeting of over a hundred Christian people here in London I asked how many present had family prayers. No one did. No one! I then asked how many people present were brought up in homes where they used to have family prayers. The show of hands indicated 10 per cent. Do you not realize that here is a serious situation? Mothers and fathers grumble to me about boys and girls in their teens and say, "They don't seem to care about the things that matter." But you parents can't have it both ways. You can't grumble that your children at sixteen don't care about the things that matter, if, when they were six, they had no reason to suppose that *you* cared about them. I feel indignant sometimes when parents whine to me and say, "Just look at John! Look at Mary! They are going wild!" Those parents forget that they themselves have remained steady only because of an anchor that was put down in *their* childhood by *their* parents, whose methods they now regard as narrow-minded, old-fashioned, and out-of-date. They are not putting down any anchor for their own children, and they don't intend to. But they grumble when those children go wrong and desert the values which their parents want them to have. A woman said recently, "I don't know what my mother would have said if she saw my children." If I had had the courage and had known her well, I should have said, "I think I know what your mother would have said. She would have told you to do the same for your children as she did for you."

b) The second thing we must do to retain the values in our home life is to maintain a definite link with some church. The City Temple has never been allied to a narrow denominationalism, and it is not now. Better to be a good Roman Catholic than a bad Congregationalist; better to be a good Methodist than a poor Quaker. Find a church which brings God most truly to your own heart, and stick to it, but don't suppose that in your home you can maintain Christian ethics when Christian worship has fallen into decay. How unreasonable many people are! They cut off their family from the origin of the world's ideals and expect the ideals to go on living. You might as well cut a limb off an apple tree in the late summer and wonder that the young fruit shrivels and dies before the autumn harvest can be gathered. The great ideals of the world were born in the Christian religion. It gave them birth. It gives them energy.

It gives them sustaining power. You cannot cut the power off and expect the ideals to go on. Yet people say, "Look at the average morality today!" But why be surprised? Their source in Christian worship has been removed. The second thing, therefore, to maintain the values essential in a healthy, happy home life is to maintain a definite link with the church of your choice.

c) The third factor by which a home is held together is healthy sex knowledge and wise action in sex affairs. Sex problems account for probably 90 per cent of the broken homes of our land, and there are so many problems that run back to sex, including a high proportion of those dealt with in our psychological clinic, that I will mention only three.

1) The sex ignorance of young people is the first problem. No parents have any right to send children into the world in their teens without making sure that they know what are politely called the "facts of life." Ideally it is best that questions should be answered when they are asked, and answered without embarrassment, avoiding the emotional setup and the hush-hush, "Now-I-will-tell-you-something" spirit. If a child says, "Mummy, what is that in the sky and how does it work?" you say dispassionately, "It's an airplane," and you tell him how it works. If he says, "Where do babies come from?" try to avoid answering with any different tone of voice. He only wants to build the facts into the fabric of his mental structure. If you spoke in the same way about airplanes as silly parents do about sex questions, the child would be as embarrassed at the sight of an airplane as he is embarrassed at the sight of his own body, or the bodies of the opposite sex, or questions about babies, and so forth. Make sex the normal, healthy, happy, holy, modest thing that God meant it to be. You will do an enormous service to your children and prevent sex from ever becoming a morbid and furtive secret surrounded by unhealthy emotion.

2) The second thing about sex that is so fruitful of broken family life is that it appears that many married women with children simply will not understand that God's way of making sure that little children are looked after is to divert much of the sex energy of the mother from the channels of physical desire to those of maternal care of the child. Fathers love their children in quite a different way. Remember how dependent a little child is on the mother before birth, during nursing, and in the early years. A woman uses up sex energies in that way to such an extent that often she does not hunger for the biological way of sex

gratification nearly as much as she did at the time of her marriage. But a man up into the fifties and sixties is just as eager for physical sex expression as the woman he married was at twenty-five. Women tend to regard physical sex expression as unclean, animal, even beastly. The fact that they do not continue to feel the same urge of desire they falsely regard as spiritual advance, and they deny their husbands physical satisfaction to such an extent that they impose on men a terrible strain and often a crippling sense of frustration that turns love to hate, secret and even repressed though the hate may be. For this reason men frequently fall into contracting all sorts of other emotional and physical liaisons out of the sheer starvation which a little understanding on the part of their wives would entirely avoid. Let there be more frankness and understanding of each other's natures in this matter, for the problem is not merely physical. It has spiritual repercussions, because if physical needs are not satisfied, there develops a spiritual separation which ends in that icy, polite tolerance of one another which is almost as bad as open hostility. Sometimes it is the woman who is sexually unsatisfied. Then let her say so. If necessary, talk the problem over with a psychologist. It is worth going to immense trouble to win physical sexual harmony.

3) The third point I would make about sex in regard to family unhappiness is that a great many married men have never understood the inwardness of Balzac's great saying about women that "a woman is like a musical instrument, and he that would draw forth harmony must learn how to play." The physical expression of sex is often practiced by men in a way which gives *them* satisfaction but leaves young wives unsatisfied. There is a technique in physical love which the Indians are sensible enough to teach their young people before marriage. Far too long we have neglected this simple but most important matter. It is not suitable that I should here outline this technique. I would urge all young married people to read the appendix to the Rev. Dr. Herbert Gray's little book *Successful Marriage* or an even more definite book, *Guide to Marriage,* by the Rev. Leslie Tizard. I would say only this, that hundreds, and probably thousands, of marriages have gone wrong from the very beginning for the simple reason that physical harmony has never been established, simply through the ignorance and ineptitude of a blundering husband who does not know, and will not learn, how to play the instrument of his choice in a way capable of winning an ecstatic re-

sponse and a joy in union, physical and spiritual, which is God's will for both men and women.

d) The fourth point I would make under the heading of how to retain the precious values in family life is to beseech parents to try to live in the same world as their children. Make the home such a jolly place by your fun and good fellowship that no other place is nearly so attractive for young or older members of the family. The day has gone forever when parents could afford to live in a haughty, superior world of their own, in which "children are seen but not heard." You parents have no right whatever to expect your child to respect you, or even love you, because you happen to be his father or mother. Far less have you any right to demand respect. You must win both respect and affection, and do so by *giving both.* When the little boy next door comes in for milk and cookies, you are ever so much nicer to him than you are to your own boy. You speak to him politely and treat him as a little grownup. You demand that your own little boy shall give you affection and respect and confidence because you happen to be his father. Remember that he did not ask to be born, and certainly he did not ask to be born into your family. Your pleasure, perhaps not even your intention, produced him. He too is a little personality with his own rights, and to develop a personality within the family is the whole purpose of the family; not that he should keep your rules, so often given "because I tell you to," without any better reason or reasonableness. Do try to live on his level. See his little problems and share them with him. Treat him as a little grownup. Here is an illustration of what I mean. I saw a father who had called to his little boy to come to dinner ("Now, come at once, Peter!") pick him up and dump him in his high chair in a very rough, rude, and peremptory manner, saying, "Why didn't you come at once?" having given him no time to finish the little building he was making with his bricks. Fortunately his mother had the courage to say, "How would you like it if, when you were just finishing writing a letter and I called you to dinner, someone three times your size picked you up and dumped you roughly at the table? You would show just as much bad temper as Peter has just shown." And I am entirely in support of the mother's attitude.

I shall never forget hearing a little girl say to her mother, "Mummy, isn't it lovely in our family? Everybody loves everybody." Now, that is a real family! There is freedom for personality to develop, but the family is a unity, and the concerns of one are the concerns of all. Ideally the individual lives—in the fullest sense of the verb—in the family, the family in the community, the community in the nation, and the nation in that world family of nations to which God's Spirit is leading us.

There is nothing finer in the world than a real Christian home, in which religion has no elements of fear or coercion, but where the mind lights up at the thought of religion as it lights up at the thought of a day's holiday in spring among the mountains. It may be worth everything to you young parents—it may save you literally years of sorrowful remorse over children gone wrong—to make the Christian religion that thing of beauty and joy, that loving relation of children with a heavenly Father, of fellowship with Christ and of possession by the Spirit of truth, which is real, undenominational Christianity.

Don't let this make no difference to what you *do*. Bring love and humor into the family atmosphere. Mind you, when you go home from church on Sunday morning, there will probably be some hostility from those who spent half the morning in bed and the other half lounging in the garden. I don't think you should be surprised at that. For one thing, the very fact that you get up early and make the trip to church on days that simply shout for the river or the woods will make those who succumb to other less strenuous allurements dislike you. They will hate the implied superiority and the implicit rebuke of your churchgoing. At the beginning of the first world war some student friends of mine who were training for the ministry joined the army. There were not enough uniforms to go round, and for fun they put on their dog collars each morning, until at last the sergeant major said, "For God's sake get these men some uniforms. They remind me of my sins every time I look at them." Yes, don't be surprised if your churchgoing makes people critical. Possibly it reminds them of their sins, of earlier habits now discarded, of youthful ideals unrealized, of glorious dreams that are dead. Of course they may have every *right* to be critical, especially if you ought to be at home on Sunday getting the dinner and doing the chores so that your mother may rest or worship. It may be, indeed, that they will accuse you of going to church but not living a life that is any different from their own, or the countless others who never worship God. But because you do go to church, go back and bring into your family environment good will, good humor, joy, and serenity of mind.

Further, if you yourself are grappling with the very problems I have been talking about, go on from where you are. Don't simply sit down and hope that everything will come right some day. It probably won't. Don't look back and say, "I wish things were different and a bit more like they used to be in my old home." Don't let husband or wife say, "I wish we could go back to the days before the war." You cannot go back, and it is no good repining. You have got to do something *now* about your situation and go *on* from the point where you are now. Of one thing I am absolutely certain: a real live Christian can bring to a very difficult family atmosphere an element which in the end will transform it. I believe that the Christian home is the hope of the nation and the only basis of that new world about which so often we dream.

XIV

Can We Get What We Want if We Pray in Christ's Name?

Whatsoever ye shall ask in my name, that will I do. —John 14:13

THAT SENTENCE CERTAINLY SOUNDS LIKE WHAT BUSINESSMEN CALL "a firm offer," an explicit promise. If we are to bank on the "promises of Holy Scripture," then surely we can bank on that.

I remember, as a boy of fifteen, banking on it. I wanted to pass an examination. I had had a religious upbringing. I read the words of our text through carefully. They seemed too good to be true. But there they were, definite and apparently unambiguous. "Whatsoever!" Surely matriculation could be included. You had only to add the magic formula "in the name of Jesus," and the thing was done! I very badly wanted to pass that examination, and I had worked hard for it. So, on the night before it began, I reminded God that Christ had promised, in his sacred word, that whatsoever we asked in his name we should have. I failed! What was worse, though I didn't think so at the time, I lost a good deal of faith. It didn't seem fair. What is the good of scripture promises if they let you down just when you want them most? The lamp flickered that time. The light almost went out.

I know now that so far from being too good to be true, the words, as they stand without intelligent interpretation, are not good enough to be true. Prayer would be like putting a coin in the slot and pulling out the bar of chocolate. And God couldn't run his universe at all if that were true. We should make an enormous mess of his world. Prayer for a quiet mind in the examination would have been answered. Prayer for the magical supply of knowledge I had not acquired and skill that I did not possess—prayer for an unethical advantage over other boys—was denied. I worked harder the next year and passed. Then in my heart I told God I could do without his promises. I could do things by myself!

It took me years to realize that when a man talks of his own powers, he really means those God has lent him. But the whole difficulty opens up some important religious truths, and I am writing these words in the hope of being able to pass on to others certain clues about the way God deals with us, because those clues have been of help to me.

What, then, are we to make of these words? Three preliminary explanations can be offered.

1. Scholars are unanimous in telling us that in the Fourth Gospel we are not to look for the exact words of Jesus, especially if there is no parallel in the other three. The Fourth Gospel was not written until A.D. 100 or 120. Jesus died in A.D. 29. No doubt the Fourth Gospel incorporates the ideas of Jesus, but the words used may be those of a mind that reverently dwelt on those ideas and, after a long period, reproduced them in words that never attempt speech reporting.

I mention this point because it is important for all interpretation of the language of the Fourth Gospel, but yet I feel uneasy at pressing it. It seems an evasion of our problem. And it seems hard to believe that such a sentence as our text would ever be written down in the best-loved chapter of the whole Bible unless Jesus said something very like it. Nor do I think we need have recourse to such a desperate expedient.

2. The second point is that the word "name" in the New Testament so frequently means "power." When the disciples went out in the name of Jesus, they went out in the power of Jesus. That idea should be kept in mind because throughout the Bible, and in Eastern life even now, it continually crops up.

Knowing a person's name is thought to give one power over that person. "Tell me thy name," says Jacob to the angel,[1] but though the angel knows Jacob's name (= has power over him), Jacob never learns the angel's name. "What is thy name?" says Jesus to the mental patient who lived among the tombs.[2] "My name is Legion," says the patient. When the latter was asked the question, he would know Jesus was seeking power over him, and in replying the patient would signify his willingness for Jesus to have that power.

Part of my own life was lived in India. There a new recruit would often refuse to disclose his name to the enrolling officer. He gave a *nom de guerre*, as it were. His own name would be in a little cylinder

[1] Gen. 32:29.
[2] Mark 5:9.

bound on his arm in case—and only in case—he was killed. Giving away his name to another meant giving himself into the power of another. So a Hindu bride's name would frequently not be disclosed, even to the bridegroom, until after her marriage. Only after he became her husband had he the right to have *power* over her.

When we say of God, "Thy name be praised," we mean "Thy power be praised." "Great is thy name" means "great is thy power." Egyptian charms and magical incantations have been discovered containing the name "Jesus" to be repeated many times. The name spelled power.

Now, with all this in our minds, can we translate our text again: "Whatsoever ye shall ask in my *power,* that will I do"?

3. Here a third point must be made. If you say, "Well, God can do everything. Everything is within his power," I must make a reply that to some may seem like splitting hairs, but I think it most important.

We are never to think of God's power in terms of what he could conceivably do by the exercise of what we may call sheer omnipotence which crushes all obstacles in its path. In a sense I suppose God *could* do anything that was not self-contradictory—like making a square circle. We are always to think of God's power in terms of his purpose. If what he did by sheer omnipotence defeated his purpose, then, however startling and impressive, it would be an expression of weakness, not of power.

Indeed, I think a good definition of power is "ability to achieve purpose." This applies to the power of a gun, or a drug, or an engine, or an argument, or even a sermon! Does it achieve its end? Does it fulfill its purpose?

Let us try to realize that God's power is not put forward to get certain things done, but to get them done in a certain way, and with certain results in the lives of those who do them.

We can see this clearly in simple human illustrations. My purpose in doing a crossword puzzle is not to fill in certain words. I could fill them in easily by waiting for tomorrow morning's paper. Filling them in without the answers is harder but much more satisfying, for it calls out resourcefulness, ingenuity, and discipline which by the easier way would find no self-expression. How much like life is that! God knows all the answers to our puzzles and so many he won't tell! We call him hard and cruel and wonder whether he exists. But finding out the answers does something for us that would not be done if he told us the answers.

Similarly, to borrow an illustration from William James, eleven men battle desperately on a field, risking falling and injury, using up a prodigious amount of energy, and when we ask why, we learn that it is to get an inflated, leather-covered sphere called a football across a goal. But if that is all, why doesn't someone get up in the night and put it there? Football games are not played to get a ball across a goal, but to get it there under certain conditions, in a certain way, with certain results in the lives of those concerned. How like life that is too! Power to get the ball across the goal is to be interpreted in terms of purposes and only makes sense in the light of those purposes.

Let me take a more serious illustration from a book by the late Lily Dougall. A woman who had been ill was adored by her husband to the point of foolishness. During her convalescence he carried her from one room to another, and on sunny, warm days he carried her to the orchard and back again. At last the doctor determined to interfere. "If you go on doing this," he said, "she will never walk again. She so likes being fussed over that she won't try to walk, and her muscles will atrophy." The husband saw the point. Subsequently he had to watch her walk, tremblingly and stumblingly. He even had to let her fall. It would have been *so* easy to have rushed to her aid. It would have looked like an expression of power. It is just what we want God to do, blame him for not doing, and doubt him because he does not do. But if the husband had intervened, it would have defeated his purpose and therefore been an expression of weakness and not of power. It was costly to hold back and to refrain, but that nonintervention was power. So God, who no doubt *could* rush in and act in the way we want, *must* not do so, for to do so would defeat his purpose. It would leave undeveloped some of the loveliest things in human nature which spiritually get us far nearer to our goal of perfection than any intervention could. Action which defeats purpose is weakness. Power is the ability to fulfill purpose. No one knows what it cost God to refrain from intervention when wicked men put his beloved Son to death. But the restraint was not weakness. The Cross was called the *power* of God unto salvation.

So now can we write down this puzzling text again? "Whatsoever ye shall ask that is in harmony with my purpose, that will I do." And God will do it in that co-operation with us which prayer always involves.

It looks, then, as if we must use our brains and try to understand what God's purposes are, for our petitions are, so to say, to be passed through the sieve of divine purpose before they can be granted. When I use the words "Through Jesus Christ our Lord" at the end of a prayer, I do not only think of him as the divine Mediator between God and man. I try to sieve my petitions through the mesh of his mind. If my prayer is in harmony with Christ's purposes, he will show me how to co-operate with him so that I may reach the goal of a desire which is his as well as mine.

That precious co-operation with him is the richest promise in our text. What God wants us to have Christ will help us to win. "Whatever God hath ordained," said Mohammed, "can be attained only by striving." And it is having Christ with us that gives us confidence to pray at all.

My mind goes back to days when my daughter was a little girl. When we went together into strange scenes, and especially strange company, how tightly she would hold my hand and cling to me until she felt at home! So I think Paul uses the phrase he loved so much, "through Christ Jesus," "in Christ Jesus." Christ had opened up a new world and called him into splendid, but terrifying, experiences, taught him to believe daring things and to ask incredible things for himself. Assured that this was God's purpose, he went forward, but it was always with his hand in Christ's—"in the name of Jesus," "through Jesus Christ." He could face even "the heavenly places" as long as it was "in Christ Jesus" he moved forward.[3]

The lines are as true today as they were three hundred years ago:

> Good and great God! How should I fear
> To come to Thee, if Christ not there!
> Could I but think He would not be
> Present, to plead my cause for me;
> To Hell I'd rather run, than I
> Would see Thy face, and He not by.[4]

Now that we have cleared the ground concerning the meaning of the words of this difficult text, let me say four things which may clear

[3] Eph. 2:4-10.

[4] Robert Herrick, "No Coming to God Without Christ."

matters up for those who, in deep dejection, wonder why God doesn't give them that for which they ask in sincere prayer.

1. *God couldn't give us what we really want if he gave us what we think we want.* After all, we are like very little children before God. Jesus encouraged us to use the key which this simile provides, when we could not understand God's ways with us. "If ye then, being evil, know how to give good gifts unto your children: how much more shall your heavenly Father . . ."

Let us imagine that you ask your little boy what he wants to be, and that when he says "an engineer" you close with him and give him his heart's desire. Engineers are splendid people and most important helpers of the community, but seven years of age is not mature enough for a person to make up his mind to join their ranks. How grateful your boy is now that when he asked to be an engineer, you did not close down all other jobs but the one he asked for!

Suppose your little child asked to be let off school, and you granted his request. How he would exult and laugh at the other boys whose fathers would not answer their prayers! But who laughs last? What irreparable harm would be done to a child debarred from any education in the modern world! Yet isn't that just what we all do? I write these words during a time of illness. I want to be well. I pray for health. Surely health is God's purpose. Surely I can claim the promise here. Surely I can do God's own work better if I am well. Surely my wife should be relieved of her constant anxiety over my recurring bouts of illness. But suppose this is an examination in the school of life, and suppose I am trying to evade it instead of passing it. Suppose passing it will qualify me to help others pass it. Suppose it would be favoritism or magic or weakness to let me out of this net that hampers me so often, a net of man's weaving perhaps and not God's at all. Still I can get comfort and strength from our text: "Whatsoever ye shall ask, if it is in harmony with my purposes, I will show you how to co-operate with me, so that together we may win it." One day we shall thank God for his refusal to answer our prayers, just as a typhoid patient on recovering might well thank a doctor or nurse for refusing to give him food. Yet he wanted food, argued that one must eat, felt affronted and irritated at the refusal. With Tagore one day we shall say to God, "Thou didst save me by Thy hard refusals."

2. The second thing we may say is this: *God doesn't give us what we want until we find the relevant way of co-operating with him.*

The best illustration I know is that of Sir Ronald Ross. He was a religious man and prayed so hard that God would help him fight malarial fever. For years his prayer seemed unanswered. He wrote:

> I pace and pace, and think and think, and take
> The fever'd hands, and note down all I see,
> That some dim distant light may haply break.
>
> The painful faces ask, Can we not cure?
> We answer, No, not yet; we seek the laws.
> O God, reveal through all this thing obscure
> The unseen, small, but million-murdering cause.[5]

Then, after much toil, research was successful, and he wrote again:

> This day relenting God
> Hath placed within my hand
> A wondrous thing; and God
> Be praised. At His command,
>
> Seeking His secret deeds
> With tears and toiling breath,
> I find thy cunning seeds,
> O million-murdering Death.
>
> I know this little thing
> A myriad men will save.
> O Death, where is thy sting?
> Thy victory, O Grave? [6]

If a man has a leg blown off, the relevant way of co-operating with God, in my opinion, is not to pray that he may grow another one, but to get him an artificial limb. Obvious, you say. But perhaps you yourself need not prayer, but a new form of treatment, or a holiday, or a friend, or a task that makes you serve others, or even just sheer courage to go forward. "Wherefore criest thou unto me?" saith the Lord. "Speak unto the children of Israel, that they go forward." [7]

[5] From "Philosophies." Used by permission John Murray, London.

[6] "Lines Written After the Discovery of the Germ of Yellow Fever." Used by permission John Murray, London.

[7] Exod. 14:15.

3. But immediately let a third thing be said: *God often could not fulfill his purpose for the individual without defeating his plan for the whole human family.*

It may well be—and I believe always is—God's final purpose to deliver his children from suffering. Suffering is evil. God does not need evil before he can accomplish his good. When good is born of suffering, it is because God brings his good out of our evil. Jesus regarded suffering as evil and therefore fought it. Of one sufferer he said, "This woman . . . whom *Satan* hath bound." [8] But maybe God cannot show you the way to health because he is waiting for the human family, and within it scientists, trained as you are not, to discover the remedy. I wonder how many diseases could be cured, or prevented, if the human family used *all* its resources to combat them. But God will not show favoritism to the individual in a way which would divert the human family from using its resources to cure and to prevent illness. You would not want your child at boarding school excused from some unpleasant experience which all the rest of the school suffered, just because he prayed to the principal and curried favor with him. The normal child would hate to be so delivered.

A frantic woman once harassed a stationmaster by asking him to hold up an express train because her husband had not arrived at the station in time and they both wanted to visit their dying son. He had the *power* to hold the train up, but he refused. "I must not answer *your* prayer," he said in effect, "and defeat the purpose of those who arranged the train to suit hundreds who depend on its running on time." [9]

Maybe in one of a hundred ways we pray to God for something which he must not grant to one because of his purpose for the many.

If that seems a hard and disappointing thing to write, I can only add my own faith that no suffering is *finally* wasted. I could not believe that God is the kind of person who lets little children suffer without *in the end* using their pain for their blessedness and his glory. We can but offer our suffering to him in that faith.

In the meantime we may remember how much we have gained from the assets of the human family. From individuals have come to us some of life's greatest blessings. Things they have invented or dis-

[8] Luke 13:16.

[9] I have borrowed this illustration from Dr. Crichton Miller, *The New Psychology and the Preacher*, p. 209.

covered, agonizing to wrest secrets from nature to human advantage: anodynes for human pain, preventions of disease, energies of nature that do the work of man. Why, we have only to run through the things we ate for breakfast this morning to realize what breakfast would be if we could use nothing but what we, as individuals, had invented, discovered, learned, or obtained!

Obtaining the advantages of belonging to the human family, some of us must suffer the disadvantages. Using the assets, we must suffer the liabilities. No individual *in the end* will deem God unjust, for justice is an eternal value. But in this world the liabilities of the family seem to fall unjustly on some individuals. They suffer for us. I love the words Carlyle wrote to one of them: "For us was thy back bent. For us were thy straight limbs and fingers so deformed; thou wert our conscript on whom the lot fell, and fighting our battles wast so marred."

4. The last point I would make is that *God never refuses to respond to our prayers.* Often, for reasons some of which we have seen, he must not respond in the way we wish, but it is incredible that there can be such a thing as prayer to which God makes no response at all. "God may not answer prayers," someone has said, "but he always answers people." God is not a store which you may ring up, and on not getting just what you ordered, trade elsewhere, though that is the way God is often treated. After all, the great saints of both Old and New Testaments did not get what they asked. Moses asked to lead his people into the promised land, but though he saw it he never entered it. Paul prayed for some handicap, which he called "a thorn in the flesh," "a messenger of Satan," to be removed. He prayed repeatedly about it. That is what the word "thrice" means.[10]

Surely it was the purpose of God to remove it and let his servant Paul serve him without handicap. He could surely do so much more good in the world. Besides, Paul healed others. How humiliating it is to be able to heal others and be ill yourself! Look at the deductions people make: "He heals others through faith, and he can't heal himself. The man's discredited. He's a fake. He hasn't got faith enough himself."

Few can guess what Paul felt about it. No one quite knows what the illness was. Some think malaria. Some think epilepsy. Perhaps it was what some call nervous exhaustion. It sounds like it in some passages: "It was in weakness and fear and with great trembling that I visited

[10] II Cor. 12:7-8.

you."[11] He speaks of "the distress which befell me in Asia," and says, "I was crushed, crushed far beyond what I could stand, so much so that I despaired even of life."[12] Then listen to this: "I got no relief from the strain of things, even when I reached Macedonia; it was trouble at every turn, wrangling all round me, fears in my own mind. But the God who comforts the dejected comforted me by the arrival of Titus."[13] In another passage he refers to "many a sleepless night."[14] All these references point, in my view, to neurosis with its horrible fears and its depression, its irrational fatigue and its insomnia, its trembling and its elusive causation. Perhaps, as is so often the case, the neurosis was superimposed on epilepsy or some other physical ailment.

Never let us imagine that the saints were always well, always high-spirited, always exuding hilarious and holy gaiety, always able to sleep at night and never haunted by doubts and fears, and that they always got their prayers answered.

Yet Paul the man was answered, and here is the answer he received. "He [the Lord] told me, 'It is enough for you to have my grace: it is in weakness that my power is fully felt.' " "So," Paul says, "I am proud to boast of all my weakness, and thus to have the power of Christ resting on my life."[15]

We are very little boys. We ask God for the wrong things. We want magic and favoritism. We want things as individuals that must wait on the family of all mankind. We want things that would make impossible our highest good. We want God to make us this and that without any effort of our own. We want him to give us what we think we want, and we cannot tolerate his slow, patient ways with us that he may give us what *he* wants and what *we* should want if we could see farther ahead. We often ask for what is ours already and only needs taking. We struggle all our lives to get our hands on "treasures" which we only have to leave behind. We fight and strive and grab and hurt others to possess things, and when we get them we think God has at last answered our prayers, and never know how he must smile in loving solicitude when we discover that their possession leaves our hearts empty and unhappy and angry at our own disquietude. We ask for what can be ours only if we

[11] I Cor. 2:3 Moffatt.
[12] II Cor. 1:8 Moffatt.
[13] II Cor. 7:5-6 Moffatt.
[14] II Cor. 11:27 Moffatt.
[15] II Cor. 12:9 Moffatt.

are willing to work with him and find the relevant way of co-operation. Perhaps we shall grow up one day and say "Give me" less and "Make me" more, and "Show me thy glory" most of all. For that is all that matters. In his glory is our blessedness, and certainly nothing else matters, either for him or for us.

Yet, little children though we be, unable to ask wisely, seizing on half-understood promises, as I did when I was a child, sobbing ourselves to sleep because the answer seems so long delayed or never to come at all, God cannot possibly make no response, and our prayer cannot be wasted if it draws us to him and helps us to know him better.

If your little child asked you for the silliest thing you can imagine, a thing that would do him untold harm, you would not avert your face, look the other way, pass him over in dead and unresponsive silence. No one worthy of the name "Father" could do that. You would most probably gather him in your arms and kiss away his tears, and do so with a warmth the greater in that you could not grant his desire. And Jesus taught us to call God "Father." On the cross, with many a petition of his own ungranted, Jesus called him "Father."

I will never believe that God is not greater and more loving than any human father, though I am ready enough to admit how hard, and often impossible, it is to see where he is leading his world and ourselves. Nor will I accept any limitations of his power except his own. Nothing can be true of him in terms of power which would contradict his nature in terms of love, holiness, and utter wisdom.

Will this omnipotent and loving Father avert his face from our foolish praying? Will he make no response of love to *us*, whatever it is we *ask*? Are we orphans on this lonely planet amid the terrifying immensities of space? Is there no one to mark our feeble footsteps as we wander in the pathetic paths of unimportant lives, crying out, however mistakenly, for love and meaning and the satisfaction which our whole nature craves?

We could bear having our prayers unanswered. We could not bear the thought that there is no response to the longing which prompts us to pray. Rather may death come soon in any manner which is certain, that we may rest at last from futile desire in a mad universe, where passionate longing is a mockery, and life as meaningless as a nightmare and as empty and hollow and unsatisfying as a dream.

But this cannot be. For God has made a response that goes on sounding in men's ears forever: a Word made flesh. God himself in loving, human form. With us once and for all in history, and with us in his Spirit day by day. He is the reality behind all men's longing. He is the certainty all men are seeking. He is the answer to all men's prayers.

> Lo, amid the press,
> The whirl, the hum, the pressure of my day,
> I feel Thy garment's sweep,
> Thy seamless dress;
> And, close beside my work and weariness,
> Discern Thy gracious form.

XV

Is It Any Good Praying About the Weather?

LET ME SAY AT ONCE, QUITE BLUNTLY, THAT I DON'T THINK IT IS. I think today's weather on the Yorkshire moors, where I am writing these words, was fixed and determined long before Yorkshire existed, and probably as soon as the contours of the earth had settled into anything like their final form. If I thought otherwise, I would have prayed for a fine day and avoided this driving rain from lowering skies, keeping me under a roof when I want to search for birds' nests and get healing for spirit, mind, and body from the sunshine and peace of a spring morning.

At the same time I will not write with intolerant dogmatism. I am sure a man can be as good a Christian who believes in praying about the weather as a man who does not. And if bad weather makes you pray when good weather would leave you prayerless, it could be argued that it is a good thing to pray whatever you pray about. It is a good thing for a child to talk to his father about *anything* that worries him.

When this question was seriously raised at the City Temple, it had a special importance in that very bad weather had destroyed a great part of the harvest, and no less eminent an authority than an archbishop had recommended prayers for good weather from every Anglican pulpit on a certain Sunday.

The matter is important in many ways:

1. If successful harvesting depends partly on faithful praying, we ought to say so and recommend prayer for good weather in the Free Churches also. I have the very deepest sympathy with the modern farmer. He is *the* most essential member of the community. Unless some men were farmers all the time, all men would have to be farmers part of the time, or die! Yet a clever, careful farmer, by an event impossible to foresee, can have his whole crop ruined and all his work undone by the weather of a few hours. The farmer exists to co-operate with God and

help God answer the prayers of his people, "Give us this day our daily bread," and God doesn't seem to care. If prayer *is* relevant, let's pray.

2. If a wet day defeats a worthy object and prayer could have prevented the rainstorm, we are to blame for not praying. I remember arranging, many years ago, a trip to the seaside for poor children. With others I took immense care to organize well. Money was collected to take to the sea children who had never seen it. Many children saved up to spend money on this day of days. At last the great day came. Instead of their being able to play on the yellow sands and make their sand castles, paddle and bathe in sunlit, dancing waves, it rained all the way there and the whole day through. The sea was a gray misery of flying foam thrashed by a merciless and bitterly cold east wind. The children disembarked from steamy busses and played games disconsolately in a desolate schoolroom not nearly so well equipped as their own at home. They ate the lunch they brought and the tea we gave them in the schoolroom, and then embarked in the busses, wiping the steam from the windows and peering at the wet, cheerless landscape until it was too dark to see anything. A miserable day was had by all. When we got home, it stopped raining. The next day, when they were all back at school—except those who had caught cold!—was one of flawless beauty and unbroken sunshine from dawn to dusk. Yet at Sunday school we taught them that God cared for them so much that the hairs of their heads were all numbered!

3. The matter is important because our deductions about prayer for the weather may be found to cover other matters as well.

In thinking this matter out, I want to make two assumptions.

1. The first is that *God is good.* I shall not stay over this, but ask you to accept it. If God is not good, then of course there is no problem in considering that often, just as a crop is ready for gathering, it is ruined by rain, wind, flood, or frost. That is just what a fiend *would* do! But, of course, we are left with a greater problem, "Where does goodness come from?" and since *we* would never ruin a man's harvest or spoil the one day at the seaside to which little children had looked forward with such happy anticipation, are we to deduce that we are better than God and higher in the scale of moral values? For we have no doubt that goodness is *the* highest moral value.

No! I cannot escape the axiom that God is good and that therefore our prayers are not to be regarded as trying to persuade a bad God to do something good, or an indifferent God to rouse himself and be kind for once because the barley is coming up so nicely and because lame Tommy Jones has never seen the sea. Prayer is communion with a good God and *a means of finding out how best to co-operate with him.*

It is because I believe this that, with due respect, I think the prayer in the prayer book about the weather is rubbish. I don't suppose my many friends in Anglican orders ever use it, but it is a pity to retain it at all. Here it is:

> O Almighty Lord God, Who for the sin of man didst once drown all the world, except eight persons, and afterward of Thy great mercy didst promise never to destroy it so again; we humbly beseech Thee that although we for our iniquities have worthily deserved a plague of rain and waters, yet upon our true repentance Thou wilt send us such weather as that we may receive the fruits of the earth in due season; and learn both by Thy punishment to amend our lives, and for Thy clemency to give Thee praise and glory, through Jesus Christ our Lord. Amen.

A worse prayer, with such false scriptural exposition, indefensibly bad theology, and sickening sentimental sycophancy, it would be hard to find anywhere.

2. The second assumption I wish to make is that *God is power.* Of course, if God cannot help the weather, there is no problem in the spoiled crops. We, then, behold the majestic Creator saying, as it were, to his children, "Of course I love you very much, and I'm sorry your harvest is ruined, but I couldn't help it. When I created the world and determined the weather, I forgot that your crops might be spoiled and your cattle die. Now the matter is beyond me. I can't do anything about it."

No! That won't do either. God is power. He who made the elements can control them. He who determined the weather could alter it. We are not concerned with what God *can* do. We are much more concerned here with what he *does* do. We seek to understand his way of working his world. Then we can decide whether prayer is the relevant way of co-operating with him or not.

I do object most strongly to those who imply that not to believe in the efficacy of prayer about the weather is not to believe in prayer, that a man is a materialistic unbeliever if he doesn't pray about the weather, and spiritually more developed and possessing a higher type of "faith" if he does.

God is power. He *could* do many things that he won't do, just as you *could* do your boy's homework for him, but if you are wise you won't do it, even if your refusal makes him stop asking you about anything.

Now we must turn to ask and answer, however incompletely, the question, How does God run his world?

We know that in many situations he works it by the co-operation of man. He has ordained so to do. One of the wisest things anyone ever said was that word of Augustine: "Without God, we cannot. Without us, God will not." God does something without which man is hopelessly beaten, but man must do something also, and without that doing on man's part God will not do any more. Many examples occur at once. God puts stone and coal and iron in the hills, but man must build and mine and smelt. God gives corn, but man must sow, reap, grind into flour, bake, and so on, if he would eat bread.

In the moral sphere God longs for man's holiness and gives him the power of Christ, the light of conscience, and the choice of good. But man must wage a weary war with evil, or none of these factors will make him good.

In the realm of healing God longs for man's health and wills it. But man must find preventives and remedies, obey the laws of health, turn the iron in the hills to steel surgical instruments and learn to use them skillfully, understand the human mind and learn how to prevent and treat its disharmonies, *and in this field he must pray*.

In all these spheres the word is "co-operate." God will do his part. We must do ours. We must learn the relevant way of co-operating with him. "Without God, we cannot. Without us, God will not."

But now turn to the weather. What is the relevant way of co-operating with God? Is it prayer? I don't think so. In the area of health *there is an interplay of minds,* and for this reason I most fervently believe in prayer for the sick. I regard it as co-operating with God on the psychical and spiritual level of the patient's personality, just as the doctor and nurse co-operate with God on the physical level of the patient's personality. Few need reminding today of the immense effect of the mind on the body. I have had, in my own ministry, overwhelming evidence of the power of prayer in assisting God's intention to heal.[1] But in the healing, I repeat, *minds* are working on one another. My mind, as I pray for Tom Jones, reaches out to God, who is Mind, and also links up with the mind of Tom Jones, even if he is unconscious of being prayed for or too ill to be told. Think of the mind-force of a thousand people in a congregation praying for a sick child, especially if they can be made to love and care! Call it telepathy, if you like. You have only named part of the machinery of mind which God uses. You have only labeled the door through which he comes. And it isn't very profound to use the smaller word "telepathy" instead of the greater word "prayer," and it doesn't explain half the phenomena regarding the amazing power of minds over bodies.

So much, in passing, for prayer for good health. But when you ask me to pray for good weather, I wonder how it can even be imagined that my mind, in contact with God's, can shift a thing that can make no mental response—like a depression over Iceland—so that my British brothers escape a wet day and my American cousins get one. If you say, "God's mind created weather in the first place and can alter it now," I am forced to ask what God was thinking about in the first place to create conditions less ideal than I can now suggest to him in my prayers.

Notice again how different is the matter of prayer about illness. Illness is something wrong that needs putting right. Prayer about the weather assumes that the weather is wrong and needs putting right. But we have no grounds to suppose that this is so. Illness is generally due to man's ignorance or folly or sin (not that of the individual sufferer, usually, but of mankind). God wants to replace ignorance with knowledge, folly with wisdom, and sin with holiness. Nothing, then, that springs from ignorance, folly, or sin can be God's ideal intention for man. Prayer helps toward such replacement and is relevant, therefore, to illness. There is no evidence that storms are in themselves evil or due to conditions which arise from man's ignorance, folly, or sin. In the area of health and morality I *know* what God's will is and can work toward it. Christ gave us the clue in both fields. But as regards the weather I have no clue as to what the will of God is. Jesus gave us no clue there. It isn't as if human factors have altered the situation, since at the forming of the world God determined the weather. In disease, human factors *have* altered

[1] See *Healing Through Prayer.*

it. Prayer for health is recommended in the New Testament, but never prayer for good weather.

The Rev. Dr. David Smith, who greatly influenced my own life when I was in my teens, was very troubled when he was a parish minister. One of his members was a farmer whose land was down by the river. It had been reclaimed from the marshes and was wet and sodden. As harvest approached, he asked his minister to pray for a long spell of hot sunshine. But another member had a farm high among the hills. As harvest drew near, he implored his minister to pray for rain, for the soil on the hills was thin and the rock only a little way below the surface. The hot sun would wither the crops unless it rained soon.

"What could I do," said the harassed minister, "but pray that both should get in their harvest?"

I think it must honestly be said that there are situations in which prayer is not the most relevant way of co-operating with God, and we must find what *is*. That is not thinking secularly instead of religiously. It is loving God with our minds. No one, if the house caught fire, would kneel and pray. The *religious* duty is to throw on water and summon the fire brigade. If I needed an urgent operation and there were only two surgeons in the place, a competent one who was a pagan and beat his wife, and a pious duffer who took his wife to church twice on Sunday and prayed every day, I would choose the pagan, not the duffer who prayed. So would you. We must search for and find the *relevant* way of getting done what we believe to be God's will. No enthusiast for prayer must pretend that prayer is the activity *most* relevant to every situation, though there can be no situation unenriched by it. The skillful *and* prayerful surgeon would be the best helper possible.

At the same time I would not have any reader deduce that man must leave the weather to God and that man can do nothing about it.

In the first place, man can develop meteorological research. By this means he can be warned of what is coming, and in certain cases he can avoid disaster. Many lives would have been saved which earthquake, volcano, and typhoon have exacted, if man had used the resources in his power to read the omens of imminent danger.

In the second place, man has in some places brought bad weather on himself by altering the vegetation. As a staff officer in World War I, I was assigned to travel from one Arab sheik to another on government duty. Where the Turk held sway, he exacted a tax on every tree. The

Arab response to this absurd iniquity was to fell every tree unless its fruit more than paid the tax. The undergrowth perished when the shade of the trees vanished. Humidity altered. Ground became unfertile. The climate changed. The removal of trees has made what was once the reputed Garden of Eden into a desert and the climate into a nightmare. Irrigation not only is making ground fertile, but will in time modify climate. To some extent, then, man can alter the weather. Some successful experiments have been made to induce rain to fall.

In trying to cope with the dangerous dust bowls, Americans planted trees in a belt a thousand miles long and a hundred miles broad, and in altering humidity, altered to some extent the weather. Julian Huxley says atomic energy could blow the icecap off the north polar region, blow the sand off the Sahara Desert, and divert the Gulf Stream! I am not competent to judge whether he is right, but we may at least see that man may increasingly modify climate and weather with the resources in his hand, and of course he may pray for power to cope better with bad weather.

In the meantime bad weather has to be accepted. Until scientific resourcefulness can change it, we have to bear it without losing faith, because we cannot change it through prayer. We must learn to cope with its seemingly hostile treatment of our plans. Such coping is part of man's age-long attempt to be the master of the world.

One of the remarkable things about Jesus was his cheerful acceptance of the way in which God ran the universe.

Dr. Fosdick has a grand sentence in his great book, *A Guide to Understanding the Bible:*

> Jesus . . . welcomed the unbending administration of the universe. In this regard he seemed to feel, long before men knew it, the steady inflexibility of God's cosmic method, its austere disregard of ethical considerations, its vast background of procedure without thought of human merit or demerit—a dependable, impartial training-ground for souls.[2]

Though I have written much about spoiled harvests, we may notice that they never fail over all the world. Before we blame God for food shortage caused by bad weather, we should consider what war has brought upon us and how much need and hunger there would be if all natural resources were readily shared and quickly transported.

[2] P. 184.

My final word must be one of wider scope. It may be the weather is important. At the moment I am writing this, it has become very important, and many have been told to pray about it. I cannot sincerely do this, but I do believe that nothing that God allows can in itself work evil for us. Not what happens to us, but our reaction to what happens is the important thing. In the Bible a most strange point of view is to be noted. Men set out all the evidence that would prove that God is harsh, cruel, indifferent, and hostile, and then, instead of drawing the conclusion, they say that it all goes to prove that God can use the appearance of apparently hostile elements in the world to further the blessedness of his children!

So don't pray it may not be wet. Take your umbrella and grin!

XVI

Is It Unchristian to Judge Others?

Judge not, that ye be not judged. —Matt. 7:1

WHAT CAN THE SENTENCE MEAN? IT CANNOT MEAN THAT WE ARE never to criticize another. We cannot honestly discuss the great figures of our own and earlier times without making a judgment about them. Are we to remain silent and make no judgment either on Hitler or on General Booth? We cannot honestly and freely talk of one another without estimating worth or its lack. Jesus himself judged the Pharisees and criticized them in a way that has made their name a reproach forever. Jesus called Herod a fox and Peter a hindrance. Paul called his judge "a whited wall." Nor can it mean that if we refrain from judging others, we shall escape judgment ourselves. No man can avoid "the great white throne" or the "silent court of justice in his breast."

I think the sentence means, "Be careful how you assess another's character, for in so doing you unconsciously assess yourself and give yourself away." Judge not, that ye be not judged by the nature of the judgment you make of others. The plank in your own eye will be obvious by your fumbling effort to get the splinter out of your neighbor's. Jesus tells us to judge, but not glibly by appearances. "Judge not according to the appearance, but judge righteous judgment." [1] To pass a mischievous or malicious judgment on another in itself judges us guilty of mischief or malice.

Notice three ways in which by judging others we give ourselves away to anyone with insight, and reveal ourselves as people who should be judged.

1. How often our pleasure at another's fall ministers to our own complacency, lulls our conscience, makes us feel not so bad after all. "At any rate, dear," said a man to his wife in my presence, as he passed

[1] John 7:24.

over the evening paper that told of the downfall of a rival, "we haven't fallen to *that!*" So we judge others and are judged by so doing.

2. How often violent protest spells repressed desire! Psychologists tell us that when they hear someone using very exaggerated language in judgment of some particular sin, they conclude that it is the speaker's own special temptation. Having resisted it, a man is unwilling to let others have its pleasures without penalty. "If I can't have the fun I've renounced, I'll see that you don't either." Possibly the exaggerated condemnation which some unmarried, elderly women pass on sex sins illustrates the point. By judging others, they judge themselves.

3. How often, on the other hand, some of us judge lightly, pass over another's sins with the secret hope—sometimes even unconscious—that he will pass over ours. Within the marriage bond, in a case I know, both husband and wife were unfaithful. She confessed. He forgave her with a charming ease that surprised her until she found out that he had been far more unfaithful to her. So we judge others lightly in the hope that they will do the same for us—and the nature of our judgment itself judges us.

I think Jesus would have us learn from these words also how very dangerous it is to judge and to criticize others. Look at three ways in which our judging is dangerous.

1. *It is so easy to forget that the person judged is a real person.* The parson is a ready example. People, as soon as they see his collar, inwardly make a judgment about him. They themselves become different. They think he is different. They assume that he has certain characteristics of piety, or smugness, or conceit, or superiority, and the assumption blinds them to the man behind the collar, and unreality in relationship is almost predetermined. I suspect the policeman is glad when he can take off his helmet and dig the garden, or be just "Daddy" to a small boy. I suspect a schoolmaster must long to escape being "judged" all the time and get away from school and be himself. I am quite sure a woman, coming out of the hospital, is glad to cease being "that case of peritonitis" and come home and cook the dinner and be "Mummy" again. The bus driver, or shop girl, or taxi driver, whom we "judge" beforehand as bad-tempered, are people like ourselves. So is the elevator man at the stores, the man who brings your coal, or punches your railway ticket, or delivers your letters, or fills your car with gas. In making premature judgments based on what people do, we obscure from ourselves what

people are, and often are judged as snobs by our judgment on others. Let us treat people as real persons and not prelabel them with a judgment that hinders good relations and obscures the fact of their humanity. The fear of being thus judged makes people unreal and hinders the flowering of the best things in personality.

2. *Judging others widens the gulf which Christian love should bridge.* Suppose that Jesus, when he was dealing with the woman who bathed his feet with her tears, had begun with a judgment on her character. She would have rushed away in shame and in despair. Suppose he had started with Zacchæus by accusing him of overcharging. Instead he began with friendship. It was Zacchæus himself who did the judging. Jesus never said a word in criticism. So that mean little extortioner changed his way of life. Had Jesus begun with criticism, he would never have won his man. Jesus did not criticize even the thief on the cross, or the woman taken in adultery.

In the right place and at the right time criticism of what people do is necessary and helpful, but let us make sure that we have *first* established fellowship and shown good will. In *that* relationship nearly anything can ultimately be said, but without it a gulf widens, and fellowship becomes impossible. It is more important that I should show my brother that I love him than that I—with my many faults—should show him his.

Many lonely people have been made more lonely by even imagining that they are constantly being judged. Many odd and awkward people have been made cranks because the community as a whole judges them to be cranks. Judge not this man as a crank, for thus you are judged to be no lover of men, and loving comes before judging. Many very famous people are very lonely. They live in the prison of those judged "great," and between them and warm-hearted, loving, lowly folk there is a gulf fixed.

3. *Our judgment of others is so likely to be unfair.* So rarely do we know all the facts.

John Wesley, with characteristic mental insight, tells a story of a man whom in his heart he condemned for many years. Wesley labeled the man contemptuously as covetous.

One day the man contributed to one of Wesley's favorite philanthropies a gift that seemed unduly small, and Wesley lost his temper and indignantly criticized the poverty of the gift.

But the man looked Wesley right in the eyes and said, "I know a man who, at the week's beginning, goes to market and buys a few cents worth of parsnips and takes them home to boil in water; and all that week he has parsnips for his meat and the water for his drink, and meat and drink alike cost him a few cents a week."

"Who is the man?" asked Wesley.

"I am," was the reply, and, incredible though it may sound, Wesley comments in his diary as follows: "This he constantly did, although he then had an adequate income, in order that he might pay the debts he had contracted before he knew God. And this was the man that I had thought to be covetous." Let us judge not, for we are judged hasty and unfair by the very judgment we make on others.

I remember reading of a prewar luxury cruise which a young girl enjoyed with her friends. The chef was an original man. Every night at dinner the ice-cream pudding would be in some new form. One night it was a model of the ship itself; another night it would be like a statue; and so on. One night it was very ordinary, and the spoiled girl complained to the captain that the chef was getting slack. She did not know that a radio message had reached the chef that his wife was very ill, and that on the night when the ice cream was so ordinary she died. Judge not that ye be not judged to be unfair and unconsciously cruel. We so hurt others, not because we mean to be cruel, but because we utter judgments without knowledge and even without imagination.

I knew a teacher in the north of England who, without asking if there were an explanation, caned every boy who was late. Having beaten one little fellow who had never been late before, the teacher learned that the boy had been to a coal mine to try to get news of his brother after a colliery explosion. The brother was brought up to the pit head dead, and, having identified him, the younger lad went to school and was late! What an awful verdict and punishment must have resulted from the teacher's judgment on himself! "Judge not, that ye be not judged."

Day after day we judge people. He is cantankerous, or cross, or mean, or ill-tempered. She is conceited, or catty, or vain, or awkward. And so on. But we do not know what unhappiness, perhaps far back in childhood, or what sorrow, perhaps a shattering disappointment of yesterday, or what actual illness of body or mind, lies behind. Let's walk warily and speak guardedly before we pronounce judgment.

But surely we cannot be expected to refrain from passing judgment on people. No, of course not, but let us do one very important thing.

Let us judge what people do, without identifying them with their actions. "Yes," let us say of a man we criticize, "he did that, but he also did this lovely thing." He is not forever to be judged as capable of only the kind of action we condemn. This is really not a distinction without a difference. We all do silly and unkind things, but we forgive ourselves, love ourselves, and believe in ourselves. We separate our real, best selves from the silly things we do. We say, "I wasn't myself that time." Let us love our neighbors as we love ourselves, and believe in their best while we criticize their worst, and believe that they can act quite differently, and see them, as far as we can, grand and true, as Christ sees them, seeing in good faith what they will yet become. Thus to see is to love, and thus to love is to draw out the best in another, just as Christ's way of looking at us draws out the best in us.

The late Dr. Alexander Whyte used to say that before you utter a judgment on another, you should ask first, "Is it true?" second, "Is it necessary?" third, "Is it kind?" [2] What a lot of malice and uncharitable gossip and poisonous talk is released because we forget those three simple rules. Why must we, when we speak even in praise of people, or hear them praised, interject that damning "but . . ." which judges some motive as unworthy, or some act as infamous?

I love the old legend about the Master which tells how, in the street at Jerusalem, he saw a crowd collected round the body of a dead dog. Nizami, the Mohammedan poet, has incorporated it into a poem. Jesus crossed the road to see what all the commotion was about,

> And found a poor dead dog beside the gutter laid:
> Revolting sight; at which each face its hate betrayed.
> One held his nose, one shut his eyes, one turned away,
> And all among themselves began aloud to say,
> "Detested creature! He pollutes the earth and air!
> His eyes are blear! His ears are foul! His ribs are bare!
> In his torn hide there's not a decent shoe-string left.
> No doubt the execrable cur was hung for theft."

So the judgment was given and was accepted, until they heard the gentle voice of Jesus, who moved from the back of the crowd and, looking at the poor dead animal, said quietly, "See what beautiful teeth he has! Pearls are dark before the whiteness of those teeth." So men judged one

[2] D. H. Barbour, *Life of Alexander Whyte*, p. 374.

woman to be a harlot. Jesus saw past the judgment to one who loved much. Men labeled Zacchæus a profiteer, but Jesus saw a son of Abraham. Everyone knows how Michelangelo ordered a misshapen lump of marble which no one else would use, to be sent to his studio, saying, "There is an angel imprisoned here, and I must set it free." The marble was judged to be rubbish till the great sculptor saw something of imperishable worth.

If we look for the worst, we shall find it. We may even let it shock us. We may even allow it to call forth our condemnation. Neither can help our fellows. If we look for the best, we shall find it; and, finding it, we may call it forth, set it free from its trammeling inhibitions, and quicken it into yet greater beauty. Let us always suspect labels and look further.

For that is what we hope God will do for us. He knows our worst. Our thoughts are open to his sight, even if we foolishly conceal them from every other friend we have. Our secret sins are in the light of God's pure countenance. He knows us exactly for what we really are. The pus and discharge of the wound, which we take such pathetic pains to hide from the world, are obvious enough to his kind but searching glance. The silly lies behind which we hide, the affectation of offensive manners, our conceits and dogmatisms and rationalizations, cannot shield us from him.

But if he sees the worst, he still believes in our best, with a belief that is infectious enough for us to catch. Hating sin with all the hatred of one who is unutterably holy, he yet loves the sinner with a love divine enough, and big enough, to get right down below all our moral anarchies, inconsistencies, and self-hating, to lift us back to the place of new beginnings where new hopes are born and old dreams come true.

He repudiates the facile judgments men have made about us, tears off the old labels, and writes a new one, "Ye are my friends." When we read it we say, "But this can never be concerning me," but then he wrote it, and wrote it not in mockery, but in faith. That is his judgment on those who receive him. We cannot go back on such a friend. So we dare not despair, dare not relax our efforts, dare not shut our hearts to his pleading, for we cannot belie such faith in us as he has. We cannot disappoint a love like that. For if, in face of that faith, we still hugged our despair; if, in face of that love, we accepted defeat, then we should disappoint the only Lover of our souls, and in our very dreams we should be haunted by that compassionate face.

XVII

Will Christ Visibly Return to Earth?

I THINK THE ANSWER TO THE QUESTION IS "NO!" BUT A LOT OF TRULY Christian people think otherwise. And always at the City Temple, when a time is set aside for general questions, we have a number about what is called the Second Coming. To any serious student concerned with this problem I would recommend the best book I have read on this subject, *The Second Advent*, written by my friend Dr. Francis Glasson.

The questions asked are usually based on a number of New Testament passages, of which I give a selection: [1]

> There be some standing here, which shall not taste of death, till they see the Son of man coming in his kingdom. (Matt. 16:28.)

> Ye shall not have gone over the cities of Israel, till the Son of man be come. (Matt. 10:23.)

> They shall see the Son of man coming in the clouds of heaven with power and great glory. (Matt. 24:30.)

It is open to the reader to suppose that by such passages our Lord intended us to deduce that he would literally come again "in the clouds of heaven" quite soon after his crucifixion.

It is open to the reader to suppose that Jesus' very real humanity rendered him ignorant of the detail of future events, and that in fact he *believed* he would thus come again, but was in fact disappointed and mistaken.

I do not accept either of these suggestions. I think that the passages quoted above, and other similar ones, were amply fulfilled by the outpouring of the Holy Spirit on the Day of Pentecost and in the subsequent amazing spread of the new cause. Many of those standing there

[1] Dr. Vincent Taylor thinks that the famous passage in Acts 1:10-11 is not authentic.

did see Christ come, long before they had gone through the cities of Israel, in a power and glory which astonished them, and in a way which achieved far more than any "coming" depending on the eye of sense, from the necessity of which Christ had patiently weaned his followers.

Adequately to discuss here the phenomena of the Day of Pentecost would take us too far afield, but we may remember that *in experience* there has been no difference, since the Ascension, between making contact with God the Father, God the Son, and God the Holy Spirit. All are gloriously at work in every spiritual experience of the soul.

Further, we may remember that, although our Lord had promised the gift of the Holy Spirit, no doctrine of the Trinity found expression in the creeds of the Christian Church until the second century.

For myself I feel convinced that between the Resurrection and the Ascension, Christ so taught the disciples the fact of his daily presence with them, apart altogether from "seeing" and "hearing," that that presence was always a reality to them, and they never thought of him as absent.[2] When Pentecost happened, what they supremely felt was that their Lord, the same dear Companion, was in some mysterious but dynamic way pouring himself out for them again and empowering them to begin their missionary ministry of telling of the love of God and the death and resurrection of his Son and doing it through his Spirit promised to them. They were to tarry no longer, for the power from on high had baptized their fellowship [3]—on which, while in the flesh, our Lord had lovingly labored for so long—and the visible Church of Jesus was born into the world.

At Pentecost to the apostles Jesus "came" with a new power and kept all his precious promises.

Second Adventists will feel disappointed at this. It takes from them a great hope that Jesus will visibly appear from heaven in great power and glory, vindicate the faith of his people, and either reign on earth or end the history of the world by some final apocalyptic drama of judgment and take his followers to the bliss of heaven, the earth being finally destroyed. It will be, they say, the day of judgment and the end of the world.

Such a view raises more questions than we can deal with here, but let

[2] I have worked this out in *His Life and Ours,* p. 322.

[3] "Tarry ye in the city of Jerusalem, until ye be endued with power from on high." (Luke 24:49.)

us look at the one before us, the visible coming of Christ, and notice some of the difficulties.

1. We must realize that, just as we do now, men of old expressed their ideas in the thought-forms of their day. They could do no other. "Inspiration" did not magically remove the limitations of the writers. It heightened their powers, but did not remove their prejudices or distortions. Everyone in their day believed in a flat earth. None of the early Christians believed that anything spiritually important could happen out of sight of Jerusalem. Consequently the thought of Christ's "return" was conceived by the Early Church in terms of a divine man coming "down" to earth from a heaven in the sky and visible by everybody who mattered! We thus have phrases about "every eye" seeing him.[4] Even a modern hymn, still sung in churches, contains the couplet:

> All who hate Him must, confounded,
> Hear the trump proclaim the day.

I need not stay to point out that such a coming would not be seen or heard by anyone in Australia! We must part at once with the idea of a human form descending from "heaven," which is no longer believed in as up in the sky, to a flat earth within sight of all the world.

2. We can dismiss the idea that Christ, having failed to win men's allegiance by the slow, costly, patient ways of love, will descend in great power and glory and frighten men into submission by the crude device of disabling their judgment and throwing out of gear their mental machinery by a display of supernatural fireworks. His temptations and his Cross teach us that he will take no short cuts to acceptance, that he has immense respect for our mental processes, that he leaves men room to doubt him and to deny him, so that their choice of him may have a value which would be lowered and debased if fear and coercion were introduced. To imagine him trying to win to himself through terror men whom he could not win by love is to deny the consistency of the nature of the risen Lord with that of Jesus of Nazareth.

3. It is impossible for the mind successfully to hold, at one and the same time, two self-contradictory ideas. Either my boy in the Navy is *coming* home, or he is *at* home with me. I cannot juggle my mind into believing that he is at home with me and at the same time direct my

[4] Rev. 1:7.

gaze to a time when he is coming. I can benefit from either of these ideas, but not from both at the same time. Of course, he can be at home for a few days and remain quietly so, and then I may celebrate the fact of his homecoming and have a feast to which I invite my friends and neighbors, and it may be that Second Adventists think of the second coming of Christ in this way. If so, the word "coming" is singularly unfortunate, for a person who is *coming* is, by that fact, not here now. If the Second Adventists mean that Christ will vindicate his power and our faith, I agree, but their language implies the "coming" of one who is, by that fact, away.

To me the most precious thought in Christianity is that Jesus is our daily Friend, that he never did leave us comfortless or alone, and that we may know his transforming communion every day of our lives. Since, therefore, I cannot live by two ideas if they contradict one another; since I cannot, at the same time, usefully think of him as both coming and here, I seize on the more useful and important thought, and, to my own way of thinking, the better authenticated one, and hold to his presence now, not his coming in the future. I believe in his future *vindication*, but all the experience of the saints, humble or exalted, points to his presence *now*.

4. It must be said that we are not at liberty to *choose* of two thoughts the one that appeals to us as more helpful. What are the facts? The facts are that the church was misled by no less a person than Paul. He found out his mistake, changed his mind, and put the matter right! These are bold sentences. Do they represent the truth?

In his earlier writings Paul talks about those who will not die, but be "caught up . . . to meet the Lord in the air," [5] a diverting if rather giddy and useless adventure! In his earliest letter (I Thessalonians) he is all for the immediate return of Christ. He upset the church to such an extent that men left their work, ceased to provide for their families. Why carry on the dull routine of existence if Christ is coming to gather his own and set up a new kingdom? Paul thought again and wrote again advising men into "the patient waiting for Christ." [6]

We do not know what made Paul change his mind, but if he had access to our Lord's words, we are not surprised at it. For after Jesus had accepted his world mission, he spoke no word that could be inter-

[5] I Thess. 4:17.
[6] II Thess. 2:1-12; 3:5.

preted to mean that his kingdom would come soon, that it was going to be easy to win men, and that his message would find speedy acceptance in men's hearts. His very language points the other way. We know that winning "the whole world" was our Lord's purpose. Part of his burden was the gradual revelation of God that he was to be the Saviour, not only of Israel, but of the whole world.[7] Granted that he would take no coercive short cuts, what a long time winning the world would take. So he spoke of leaven working slowly and quietly and taking a long time to leaven the lump. So he spoke of seed growing secretly and quietly and taking a long time before the harvest is come. So he spoke of the Gentiles and the "other sheep" and the persecution and weary travail that lay ahead before the new world could be born. His own missionary message by itself is evidence enough that he never contemplated a sudden victory and the end of his task of winning the stubborn hearts of men.

The fact that this is the right interpretation is proved by what actually happened. There *was* no sudden advent in terms of flaming heavens and apocalyptic splendors. There *was* something far more valuable, far more like him, and far more significant. His church was born in the hearts of a fellowship of men who, on Good Friday night, were convinced that all was over and every hope dead. That church began to spread in spite of and through persecution, so that, though the might of Rome fell and the culture of Greece decayed, it grew in strength and numbers. And *still does*. For do not let us ever, because of some temporary disappointment anent the fortunes of our local chapel or denomination, forget that there are more people in the world today who love him than there ever were before, and that in India, China, and Africa the church is growing with a speed and care which should put heart into us and make us look at wider horizons than our little Bethels, with their empty seats and sometimes petty-minded gossipers who have never had any vision of what Christianity really is, and who would have irritated Paul, let alone us, with their miserable and parochial caricature of that glorious thing called the Christian religion, a caricature which cannot but repel any young man or young woman whose blood is still red.

Actually we are celebrating the Second Advent every time a heart is opened to Jesus' coming (though I would rather call it the "thousand and second advent"), every time a good deed is done in his name, every

[7] I have worked this out in *A Plain Man Looks at the Cross*.

has released were dedicated to the highest good of all. But faith demands that we believe it will be so one day and that man will see built on earth the Eternal City. We may not see it from this side. But we may, from the unseen, be allowed to go on helping to build it on earth. He shall perfect that which concerneth us. He shall complete that which he hath begun.

For myself I will not look for some coming of Christ in oriental splendor, or in some way which would contradict all I have learned of him from the Bible, the saints, and my own meager and poor but precious experiences of his ways with men. I know there is grandeur in God, and majesty and might. I know he dwells in light inaccessible, and that his being is in one way terrifying. Yet if Jesus is a true picture of God, as I believe, it is his meekness that is terrible and his humility that is awful and his love that is the light I cannot bear. I cannot believe that he who died for love will resort to terror, and that he who knocks at the door of the heart will at a Second Coming break it in. Yet I believe he is always coming.

How silently, how silently
 The wondrous gift is given!
So God imparts to human hearts
 The blessings of His heaven.
No ear may hear His coming,
 But in this world of sin,
Where meek souls will receive Him still,
 The dear Christ enters in.

And I think I can celebrate the second and the millionth advent if I keep so close to one who is always here that I respond to every loving pressure of his spirit on my own, and dedicate my days—long or short—and my strength, which in the strongest is but feeble, to the extension of his glorious kingdom in the hearts of men.

XVIII

Did Jesus Believe in a Day of Judgment?

It is popularly believed that Christianity teaches that when a man dies he sleeps until "the general resurrection on the last day"; that on this last day (a thing impossible to imagine) the world will come to an end and that those living until that time, and those dead long before it, will all be summoned to a bar of justice; that Christ, the Judge, will try them, separate them "as a shepherd divideth his sheep from the goats," and send the former to bliss unending and the latter to endless hell.

If this were the teaching of Jesus, we should have to accept it and reverently try to solve the many problems which such a view opens up. After much careful study, however, I do not believe that this is the teaching of Jesus at all, or that reliable scholarship could be quoted to sustain it as such.

There is no evidence, for instance, in the teaching of Jesus that at death men drop into a long sleep. Jesus told the dying man on the cross next his own that, that very day, they would be together in paradise. If one were fast asleep, the meeting would be valueless. At his transfiguration Jesus spoke with Moses and Elijah, who apparently were not "resting in their graves till the resurrection," and Jesus spoke of Abraham, Isaac, and Jacob in a manner that suggests that they were anything but asleep.[1]

As I understand our Lord's teaching, it is that at death men pass into a spiritual mode of existence, going on spiritually where they left off on earth. Material possessions are left behind; fame and power and social position fall away. But the accident of death neither makes a man a sudden saint nor marks his inescapable doom in hell. Man is in heaven or

[1] Luke 20:38. I have always wondered why we have for so long believed that Jairus' daughter was dead when Jesus said she was only asleep (Matt. 9:24).

hell according to his capacity—or the lack of it—to enjoy spiritual realities.

The idea of an assize seems to be based mainly on the parable of the sheep and the goats in Matt. 25. But scholars are all but unanimous in agreeing that Matthew borrowed here from the book of Enoch [2] in order to describe a philosophy of history relevant to the nations, not an assize relevant to the judgment of the individual at "the last day." [3]

It is hard to believe that a line can be drawn so finely between individuals that those on one side of it are worthy of everlasting bliss and those on the other of everlasting punishment. It is easy to see, on the other hand, that a judgment of the *nations* not only is possible, but has in fact taken place. Those which could not be used as agents of God's purpose have already passed into agelong punishment. Fourteen out of the twenty-one civilizations which this old earth has known, Toynbee tells us, have disappeared. One wonders whether Rome, Greece, Babylon, Nineveh, Mexico, Egypt, Sumeria, Persia, Byzantium, and the rest will ever know again the glory that once was theirs.

I am not, of course, saying that the words of Jesus in Matt. 25 were not spoken by him. The lovely "inasmuch" sayings seem very like him, but I am suggesting that while the parable is relevant to a judgment of the nations, no deductions about a judgment day for individuals can be drawn from it.

Can we then dismiss the idea of judgment? By no means. There is no doubt at all that the "great white throne" of the Apocalypse represents an inescapable fact. We can dismiss only the idea of a great assize and a dramatic trial and sentence of individuals. I am interested to note that Henry Drummond came to this conclusion as early as 1888.

> He did not think there would be any bar, or any trumpet, or the machinery of a human event. These would be unnecessary, because a man would know whether he was fit to live in that world the moment he was brought into contact with it. The moment a man submitted his soul to God's friends he would see at a glance instinctively whether he was fit to live in that company or not. The moment he came into contact with Christ—there was the judgment.[4]

[2] Matt. 25:32. Cf. Enoch 62:5, 11; 63:2; 102:3; 108:5, 6; and so forth.

[3] See H. R. Mackintosh, *Immortality and the Future*, p. 59; Joseph H. Leckie, *The World to Come*, p. 110; Burnett H. Streeter, *Immortality*, p. 197; L. Dougall and C. Emmet, *The Lord of Thought*, p. 170.

[4] Prin. Sir Geo. Adam Smith, *Life of Henry Drummond*, p. 281.

I agree. I believe that God has so made man that man will judge himself. Indeed, is any judgment of value to the individual unless he sees its justice and identifies himself with its findings? The highest court of justice is in the heart of a man after the light of Christ has illumined his motives and all his inner life.

Here is the inwardness of some of Tennyson's loveliest lines:

> [He] ever bears about
> A silent court of justice in his breast,
> Himself the judge and jury, and himself
> The prisoner at the bar.[5]

Christ is not so much the Judge as the Light in which we pass judgment on ourselves. Paul wrote: "When the Lord comes He will bring into the light of day all that at present is hidden in darkness, and He will expose the secret motives of men's hearts." [6] The Fourth Gospel reminds us that he did not come into the world to condemn the world, but that "this is the judgment, that the light is come," [7] and that he is the "light of the world." [8]

I may not know in the dark whether my study is dusty or not, but when I turn on the light I need no evidence but sight. I need no one else to make a solemn pronouncement. This is the judgment that the light has come. I cannot then escape coming to a true conclusion. I do not depend upon another's judgment, nor is any bluffing possible.

The truth is that every day our deeds and words, our silence and speech, are building our character. *Any day which reveals this fact is a day of judgment.* Everybody who has stayed for a time in a hotel knows the shock he gets when his bill is presented. He has previously worked out how much it is likely to be, and always finds it is more! So much a day, they said, when he booked his room, and after ten days he asks for his bill. Lo! it is far more. Then the books are opened and the bill compared with them. Then he recalls that he had two friends to dinner one night, had tea brought up to his room one wet afternoon, had a long-distance telephone call put on the bill . . . and here is the result. "I saw the dead,

[5] "Sea Dreams." Browning has the same idea in "Christmas Eve." Dowden says, "Browning's *Judgment Day* dwells wholly in the inner experiences of a solitary soul" (*Life of Browning*, p. 136).

[6] I Cor. 4:5 (J. B. Phillips' translation).

[7] John 3:19 Revised Version.

[8] John 8:12.

small and great, stand before God; and the books were opened: and another book was opened, which is the book of life: and the dead were judged out of those things which were written in the books, according to their works."[9]

We imagine our character to be one thing, but we forget that we did this and that perhaps unworthy thing, said this or that, shirked this duty and that, and that it has all added up to a total character as yet unrecognized.

> The ghost of forgotten actions
>   Came floating before my sight,
> And the things that I thought were dead things
>   Were alive with a terrible might;
> And the vision of all my past life
>   Was an awful thing to face,
> Alone with my conscience sitting
>   In that solemn silent place.[10]

Many will be surprised the other way when the books are opened. They are finer than they think. When finally the bill comes in and in the light of Christ we see ourselves, there will be many surprises. But Christ is not so much the Judge as the Light by which we judge ourselves.

Man need never be in doubt as to whether a thing is right or wrong. To know whether it is right or wrong he has only to imagine Christ standing near him as he does the contemplated thing. This is the judgment; the light has come. Man can never turn the light out and move again in a darkened world. Christ has illumined all our values, and in his light we judge ourselves.

And any day when we waken to the fact that we are making a great moral decision, any day of spiritual insight and challenge, any day of experienced nearness to Christ, any day when, in the light of Christ, we see ourselves, is a day of judgment.

Certainly the day of death will be a day of judgment, for surely then a clearer light from Christ beats upon the soul. Surely when the material things and the false values are left behind we shall judge ourselves as to whether or not we belong to the true values and have a part in the spiritual splendors.

There is a well-known story of a critic who walked round a famous art

[9] Rev. 20:12.
[10] Charles William Stubbs, "Conscience and Future Judgment."

gallery and looked at the works of the great masters and allowed himself to make a disparaging remark about them to one of the attendants. "I don't think much of your pictures," he said.

The attendant, a humble man, but a man who had come to love every picture in the gallery, made a superb reply. "Excuse me, sir," he said. "The *pictures* are not on trial."

When we confront great art and do not like it, we judge ourselves in the light of it. There can be no bluff about our judgment. If another judged us, we might resent it or make pretense. But in our heart of hearts we know whether we have a part in great art or not. The same is true of great music. The same is true of any expression of real beauty. *You* are the judge as well as the judged. The great beauty around you provides the light in which a true judgment is made.

So when we pass from this world of unreality and bluff, this place where false values blind us and where men spend their strength on worthless quests, in the light of heaven of which Christ is the Sun we shall need no great assize. "Ourselves the judge and jury, and ourselves the prisoners at the bar." Some will say, "Then I wasn't deceived. My feeble faith *is* vindicated. This *is* the reality for which I quested; here at last is that for which I looked and longed." They will send themselves to heaven. They will go to their own place. That is where they belong.

Others who have trusted to the things of this earth, who, indeed, have let selfishness rule them and allowed their character to deteriorate, will find that there is nothing to enjoy. As we say in our colloquial way, they will feel "out of it." They are in a great art gallery, but art means nothing. They are at a great concert, but music jars them. They are at a feast, but they have no appetite. They are among the saints, but they have nothing in common which makes fellowship a delight. They have sent themselves to hell.

"What of the heathen?" some will ask. In olden days missionary advocacy was urgent because men truly believed that those who did not hear the good news of the gospel were doomed to hell. We must not believe that God is as unjust as that. Those who responded to the light they had will be ready in the next world to make the fuller response to the fuller light, and

> All the love of Jesus learn
> At His feet in Paradise.

WHEN THE LAMP FLICKERS

There is a way for man to rise
   To that sublime abode:
An offering and a sacrifice,
A holy Spirit's energies,
   An Advocate with God:

These, these prepare us for the sight
   Of holiness above:
The sons of ignorance and night
May dwell in the eternal Light,
   Through the eternal Love!

XIX

Did Jesus Believe in an Endless Hell?

THIS QUESTION IS ALSO ONE THAT IS PUT FORWARD WHENEVER questions are invited, and with it another, "What did Jesus really mean by hell?" Let us look at the subject as completely as we can.

First of all, the question at the head of the page can, in my opinion, be answered negatively at once, and this for several reasons.

1. There is no word used in the New Testament which warrants us in supposing that Jesus believed in an endless hell. The Greek word translated "everlasting" [1] in Matt. 25:41 could be translated "agelong." Our word "æon" is derived from it. Tennyson transliterates it when he talks about the time it takes to change the contour of the earth's surface:

> But I should turn mine ears and hear
>
> The moanings of the homeless sea,
> The sound of streams that swift or slow
> Draw down *Æonian* hills, and sow
> The dust of continents to be.[2]

Similarly, we speak of the ice age and the stone age. We mean a long time. We do not mean any period that can be exactly determined by a figure. But we certainly do not mean an endless period.

Further, whatever meaning the concept of time may have in the next world, it is incredible that it means numbers of years going on forever. We have to use language about the next world that implies time because we here are imprisoned in time and cannot imagine what life is like outside the prison, of either time or space. But if time has no meaning, or a different valuation, the word "endless" cannot have the meaning we ascribe to it while we are within the time-prison.

[1] *αἰώνιος*.

[2] *In Memoriam*, xxxv.

The same word is used in Matt. 25 about punishment as about life. The wicked are said to pass into *eternal* punishment and the righteous into *eternal* life. But the latter may well mean a state of joy which itself passes into a far higher type of final blessedness. No one is ready for the highest possible bliss at the moment of dying, and there is no difficulty in accepting the word "agelong" for both "punishment" and "life."

2. This brings us to notice the phrase "eternal punishment." If "eternal" meant "endless," the phrase would be self-contradictory, for "punishment" is not a concept which implies only retribution or a kind of divine revenge. As Shelley said in his *Essay on Christianity,* "All the arguments which have been brought forward to justify retribution fail, when retribution is destined neither to operate as an example to other agents nor to the offender himself." [3] Punishment is a concept that implies making the wrong-doer a right-doer. When the state punishes an offender, not only is the punishment retributive and deterrent, but surely its main purpose is to make him a useful member of society.[4] The schoolteacher should "punish" to make the bad boy a good boy. The ideal of punishment is to make punishment unnecessary. Endless punishment cannot possibly do that. We can bear punishment, or, what is harder, the thought of the punishment of others, only if we believe it will achieve an end which makes suffering worth while. If hell is endless, it is valueless. If punishment is endless, when is its victim to have a chance of becoming good? His condition is hopeless. Punishment often leads to penitence and a new beginning. But when can the victim of an endless punishment begin again? Suffering from which nothing can be learned, nothing gained, is meaningless, and he who inflicted it would be a fiend, not a father.

3. This leads us to a third point which by itself answers the question. We shall see in a moment that the fact that God is love does not mean that God is soft and sentimental with us, or that he takes a lenient view of sin. Sin is the most dreadful fact in the universe. But at the same time God is a Father, and Jesus not only called him by that name, but taught men that they could best understand him in terms of that figure.

No father, whatever his child did, would go on punishing him for the rest of his life. Yet that would be merciful compared with the action of a God who, for sins committed over even a long period of human

[3] Vol. I, p. 271 (Forman ed.).

[4] The phrase "capital punishment" is, in my view, misleading.

life—which, after all, is brief in the perspective of eternity—punished his child endlessly. We can hardly suppose a thing true of God for which a man would be put into jail or into a criminal lunatic asylum. "If *ye* then, being evil, know how to give good gifts unto your children: how much *more* shall your heavenly Father give the Holy Spirit to them that ask him?" [5]

No wise father seeks to win his child by a fear motive. It is right to reverence God and to have awe in our hearts when we think of him. It is right to "fear" him in that sense: to fear sinning against him when we realize what sin is, how it wounds him, hinders him, hurts others, and does desolating damage to ourselves, separating us from him and setting up a deterioration of character in ourselves which makes us less and less sensitive to our danger and to the glory of the spiritual world. But a cringing, sycophantic fear is unworthy in us and not asked for by him. Like a human father God does not want to "win" us by that method. Like a human father he would rather fail. God would not win us by a method which, on either our part or his, denies the nature of the relationship into which he calls us.

It is a mistake to suppose that the destiny of the soul is settled at death. No authentic New Testament word can be quoted to support the idea. The earth life is of immense importance. A man's university life is of immense importance. If he slacks and takes only a pass degree when hard work would have won him first-class honors, he may not return and take his examinations again. He must remain a pass-man for life. Perhaps the parable holds. Perhaps the effect of what we do in life's lowest form at school labels us in one sense forever. Further, at death our spiritual tendency—the way we are going—is revealed.

But life goes on. And where there is life, there is always the chance of growth. Some people in this life have never had any real chance of graduating spiritually, just as many have had no real chance of education. If there is life after death—as I most earnestly believe—there must be the chance of turning to God and growing in spiritual power, beauty, and grace. Dives, in Jesus' parable, was in torment, but he ceased to be wholly selfish. He could not go back and help the old beggar by his gate, but he developed a great concern about his brothers.[6] What is described as torment has meant immediate spiritual growth.

[5] Luke 11:13.
[6] Luke 16:27-28.

Jesus took the idea of hell from the Valley of Hinnom (Gehenna), where the refuse of the city never ceased to burn. Hence the "fires" of hell. But what was foul was purified by fire, and what was previously useless was used in making roads. It is not like God to waste anything. Browning strikes the right note in *The Ring and the Book* when he describes hell as

> That sad obscure sequestered state
> Where God unmakes but to remake the soul
> He else made first in vain; *which must not be.*[7]

Hell is not to be thought of as a place, but a state of mind. Truly Milton was right in saying:

> The mind is its own place, and in itself
> Can make a heaven of hell, a hell of heaven.[8]

It is a state of unspeakable sadness, the nature of which we shall study. But belief in the character of God and his revelation in Christ forbids that it is a state of endless hopelessness. We are not to think of it in terms of punishment meted out by an angry God, so much as in terms of the consequence of living sinfully in a moral universe, through which laws operate just as inevitably as they do through the physical universe. If a man, by not looking where he is going, walks over a cliff edge and breaks his leg, we do not say, "What a terrible punishment an angry God has meted out to him!" We say, "Why didn't he look where he was going?" Hell is a state of mind reached through not looking where we are going spiritually. Spiritual law operates as certainly as the law of gravitation. We never break law. If we act as though law did not exist, we get broken. The man who walked over the cliff did not break the law of gravitation. He proved it.

After all, the universe is God's and exists for his ends, not ours. If we sin continually, we lose the power of spiritual sensitiveness. And to experience hell is to wake up to what we have done, as in a hospital the man in our illustration wakes up to what he has done. But if things have not gone too far and the desire to recover is there, healthy recovery is possible in both cases.

[7] Italics mine. From "The Pope," *The Ring and the Book.*
[8] *Paradise Lost.*

Let us put the matter in a simple illustration. Two men go to a concert of classical music. One is a musician to his finger tips. He has given hours to studying and practicing music. Every phrase of the music gives him delight, and in the concert he is, as we say, in the seventh heaven. His friend is frankly bored. He has never liked music, never taken any interest in it. He longs for the intermission. He can enter into *its* delights! They sit together, but between them there is a great gulf. And it is "fixed," for the musician cannot, however desirous, bring his friend into the bliss which his appreciation of music has made possible for him. At the same time the unmusical man *can begin to learn music.*

We pass, I think, at death into a spiritual existence, and we go on where we left off. The mere fact of dying will not make us saints. If we love spiritual things, we are in heaven. But it must be hell to be in a purely spiritual existence and find that one has lost one's taste for spiritual things and yet there is nothing else to enjoy—not even an intermission!

I don't mean to imply by the word "spiritual" only those delights which we associate with the word "religion." Religion is the highest form of spiritual experience. But a love of beauty, truth, and goodness; kindness, love, admiration for the noble and fine in character. All these things practiced in the earth life must give the soul some faculty for enjoyment of the delights of heaven. Heaven is not merely "religious" in our narrow sense of the word. No one would want to be in a heaven that was like an endless church service! But material, meretricious, and accidental advantages—like cleverness, social position, money, fame—will count for nothing. And as Jesus said, there will be many surprises.

What, then, is hell?

1. It must include the sense of deprivation. All around us, let us imagine, people revel in spiritual joy. But we were never interested in God and never bothered, and now the things we did enjoy do not exist, and what does exist we cannot enjoy. We wake up to find we are separated from God, and not only cannot find him, but *cannot want to.*

2. It must include remorse. If only we had listened when voices we scorned spoke of the things that belong unto peace. If only we had got our sense of values right and had not spent all our energies on worthless things.

3. It must include sorrow. If only we had known that sin wounded

the Man who loves us most, and hindered his plans for us and for others.

I remember Studdert Kennedy telling a story of a drunken man who used to beat his little boy. One day the little boy was lying ill and delirious, and the father for once was sober and was leaning over the cot. In his delirium the little boy put his hands up in front of his face and screamed, "Don't let him hit me, Mummy." The father realized what he had been doing while he was drunk.

Hell is the discovery that we were so intoxicated with the world that we struck out at him who loved us more than words can tell; by sin we have cut ourselves off from fellowship with the greatest Lover of our souls.

4. It must include a sense of the harm we have done others. Whether we can watch the earth life from the next world no one knows. But at some point we must, I think, realize just what our sins have meant in terms of injury and suffering to others.

5. It must be hell to realize that continued sin has meant the progressive deterioration of character. As we think of sin, we must include not only sins of commission, but of omission, of indifference to human need, of silence instead of protest, of complacency instead of action. Heaven must be the state of mind in which we utterly forget ourselves, and love to serve others, and thus to offer worship to God. Hell must be an inability to forget oneself, a hatred and loathing of self, and a despair of impenetrable gloom. Yet the despair is our chance. Despair of self leads to a chance of the Redeemer to save. "Man's extremity is God's opportunity." I cannot believe God leaves a soul in hell if there is the faintest longing for better things.

But suppose a soul endlessly turns from the light, endlessly says "No" to God. Suppose pride and selfishness remain and are never broken down by love. If a soul remains a soul, it will have the power of *choice* and be able to refuse God. Suppose it does so. Will not hell endure forever?

Theoretically yes, but I think the *endless* choice of known and recognized evil in preference to good is unlikely. If so, it is hard to escape the feeling that the Redeemer's work is imperfect. The mind cries out for *all* men to be saved. He "will have all men to be saved, and to come unto the knowledge of the truth." [9] Is the utmost glory of heaven really bliss for a devout mother if her son can never share it with her and is

[9] I Tim. 2:4.

finally lost? "Do you think that I care for *my* soul if my boy be gone to the fire?" [10]

The theoretical possibility of such an event must be allowed to logic, even though denied by faith and hope and love. In such a case my own view is that the soul disintegrates and ceases to be a personality. This may be the second death to which the Bible refers.[11] "We keep open," says C. W. Emmet, "the solemn possibility that final dissolution will be the ultimate end for such souls as have completely lost the power to recognise and desire goodness and respond to the love of God." [12] Logically any organism which ceases to have the power of corresponding with its environment perishes, and this may even be a possibility in an "immortal soul." The wages of sin, long continued and never repented, is death.

It is comforting to quote one of Browning's loveliest passages, in which he paints the picture of a fire that looks as if it were out:

> Beneath the veriest ash, there hides a spark of soul
> Which, quickened by love's breath, may yet pervade the whole
> O' the gray, and, free again, be fire.[13]

When we look at a derelict human life and think there is nothing left in it to respond to God, his loving eye may yet detect the spark divine, and the breath of his spirit may kindle it once more to life and fire.

Sin is a terrible thing, the blackest thing in the universe. Let us never forget that though the idea of hell was caricatured in a fantastic vulgarity by the generation of our great-grandfathers, we are doing our own generation a greater disservice if we are making light of sin and pretending that it does not matter, that we are "all going to the same place," and that God will pat everyone on the head at last and say, "There, there, it doesn't matter. I'm sure you didn't mean it. Go and enjoy yourself!"

We need to remind ourselves that it was Jesus who gave us the Christian teaching about hell, that the most terrible things ever said about sin were said by the tenderest lips in the world. It was *he* who spoke of the shut door [14] and the outer darkness [15] and the unquenchable fire.[16]

[10] Tennyson, "Rizpah."
[11] Rev. 21:8.
[12] *Immortality*, p. 216.
[13] *Fifine at the Fair.*
[14] Matt. 25:10.
[15] Matt. 8:12.
[16] Mark 9:43.

In the most winsome of all the parables we read, "This my son was *dead*, and is alive again; he was *lost*, and is found." "Dead!" "Lost!" So *that* is what Jesus thought of sin!

When that has been recognized, we can add this triumphant word: Christ, that great Seeker of souls and Believer in men, will never sit down contented on the throne of his glory if there is one coin bearing the image and superscription of the King lying in the dust of evil, if any seeking on his part can restore it. And that great Shepherd of the sheep, who cannot bear the thought of a one per cent loss, will never abandon his search if there is one sheep still capable of hearing his voice and responding to it, out on the cold, dark mountains, helpless, hopeless, and alone.

XX

Why Did Not Jesus Tell Us More About Heaven?

Sometimes people sneer at such a question. "Let's get on with all there is to do in *this* world," they say. "Religious people are always dreaming about another. They suppose that in another world everything will be put right, injustice corrected, righteousness rewarded, sin punished. By imaginatively dwelling on some future heaven they repudiate the demands and challenges of earth. They live in a fool's paradise."

Well, of course anyone who lives in a fool's paradise is a fool. Frankly I have not met the kind of person described. I find that some of the people doing most to straighten out things on earth are those who believe with Paul that their "citizenship is in heaven," [1] and that those who are playing the most manly part in this life say that they cannot make sense of it without the thought of another.

So the late Dr. Temple said in a letter, "For myself, I do cling to it [life after death] immensely. I do not mean that I want it for myself as mere continuance, but I want it for my understanding of life." [2]

Frequently those who unceasingly serve their fellows here began to do so for the sake of one who passed to where, beyond these clamorous voices, there is peace.

A great number of people, however, are deeply interested in the next phase of existence. The immense vogue of Spiritualism proves that. Thousands have lost dear ones and want to know the answer to innumerable questions concerning them. Thousands, if they were honest, would admit that they are getting genuinely tired of this world and look forward to another, where there will be no bodies to ache or suffer, and no queues to stand in, or forms to fill out, or taxes to pay.

[1] Phil. 3:20 Revised Version.
[2] Frederic A. Iremonger, *William Temple, His Life and Letters*, p. 626.

On the other hand many are afraid of death. Some for psychopathological reasons. They have witnessed in childhood the death of a dear one, or seen some loved form lying white and still and unresponsive, or heard some terrifying story of death. The childhood's fear has never been outgrown though its original cause may have been forgotten. Few are cowards, but many say that the fact that the next phase of life is so uncharted a sea frightens them. Always the unknown has frightened men. With Shakespeare they think with dread of

> The undiscover'd country from whose bourn
> No traveller returns.

With Shelley they ask wistfully, "Whoever yet returned to teach the laws of death's untrodden realm?"

If only someone with authority would tell! Lazarus surely must have spoken some word, but it is unrecorded. Doesn't the Bible say he was four days dead?

Alas! how uncertain we feel about the whole story! It is recorded only in the Fourth Gospel, written latest of all, perhaps later than A.D. 100, and never to be regarded as having quite the same accuracy of detail as the first three. Some critics think it was a story going about and was written in a margin of a manuscript, and copied later into the text by some enthusiastic copyist. They say that if it had happened, Luke the doctor, who would have been intensely interested, would not have missed it. Others say that Lazarus was in a state of deep trance which he could not overcome.[3]

But even if—as is quite possible to the divine Son of God—Lazarus was raised from the dead, there is no record of any report which he gave of what lies on the other side of death. Tennyson wrote:

> Where wert thou, brother, those four days?
> There lives no record of reply,
> Which telling what it is to die
> Had surely added praise to praise.

. . . .

[3] See the interesting speculation made by Yeats Brown at the end of his book *Bengal Lancer.*

Behold a man raised up by Christ!
The rest remaineth unreveal'd;
He told it not, or something seal'd
The lips of that Evangelist.[4]

An ancient tradition says that Lazarus remained a sad and melancholy man to the end of his days. Perhaps Jesus wept at his grave not only out of deep human sympathy with those who mourned, but because, to comfort them and prove the power of God, he had had to call back a spirit to the prison of the flesh when it was on the very threshold of a life more glorious and free than words can tell. The words of Longfellow's *Hiawatha* come to mind:

Come not back again to labor,
Come not back again to suffer,
Where the Famine and the Fever
Wear the heart and waste the body.

Perhaps Jesus felt like that about Lazarus.

How hard it is to get evidence! Sir Frederick Treves, once a physician to the king, thought he had obtained evidence. In his reminiscences [5] he tells of a man undergoing an operation. The patient took the anesthetic and then collapsed. He was supposed by two surgeons and the anesthetist to be dead. The pulse stopped. The heartbeat could not be felt. The countenance was like death. Then various means were resorted to, and after the longest time in Treves's experience life trickled back. Treves watched carefully. He writes:

> If the presence of life be indicated by certain manifestations, that man was dead. It seemed to me that this man must have penetrated so far into the Valley of the Shadow of Death that he should have seen something of what was beyond, some part at least of the way, some sight of the country on the other side. The door that separates life from death was surely opening. Had he no glimpse as it stood ajar? . . . The patient became conscious slowly. His eye fell on his nurse. He recognized her with a faint smile.

Treves bent over him on the other side, determined to hear every word. Would there be a word about the country beyond death?

[4] *In Memoriam*, xxxi.
[5] P. 172.

"Nurse," said the patient, "you never told me what you heard at the music hall last night."

Eagerly Treves questioned him. He remembered nothing. He dreamed nothing. He could make no report.

Many will say at once, "There *is* evidence. Spiritualism has obtained it. The next life is certain. We can get into touch with the dead. They tell us what they are doing. The mystery is solved." I am only a student of Spiritualism. I have read a great deal of the best literature, and I have attended several séances. Frankly I am very impressed with the strength of the arguments and evidences which go to show that contact is sometimes made with the dead. Up to that point I think Spiritualists have established their case.

But my difficulties are many. No one who has read the life of Harry Price can doubt that much "evidence" is fraudulently obtained.[6] No one who has studied telepathy [7] can doubt that some "spiritualistic" experiences can be accounted for without the spiritualistic hypothesis. But more devastating than all other arguments is the fact that Spiritualism has never made any contribution to our understanding of the nature of life after death which even approaches the sublimity of that implied in the New Testament. On the contrary, it has made a picture of life there which seems crude and materialistic, as when Sir Oliver Lodge's dead son Raymond talks of smoking cigars and drinking whisky and soda, living in houses made of stone and brick with glass windows, reading books, and so on.[8] And surely Sir Oliver was among the most trustworthy students of Spiritualism.

In my experience many who have consulted mediums have been bitterly disappointed. Some have felt snubbed or hurt by messages that have come through. Many have been comforted. But many have been mentally disturbed. I would recommend disinterested students to study the phenomena; but unless bereaved people are emotionally very stable, stolid, and balanced, I would not advise them to turn to Spiritualism in order to assure themselves that their loved ones are living, or to try to learn what life is like in the next phase.[9]

In desperation for news from beyond Christians may well argue thus:

[6] *Fifty Years of Psychical Research.*

[7] As in Whately Carrington, *Telepathy,* and Ehrenwold, *Telepathy and Medical Psychology.*

[8] Sir Oliver Lodge, *Raymond,* pp. 197-98, 209.

[9] I have set forth the argument for personal immortality in *The Resurrection and the Life,* and also in *After Death.*

"We believe in one who rose from the dead and, in any case, lived in heaven before his incarnation. He is a traveler who *did* return. It is not an undiscovered country to him. He *could* have spoken of 'the laws of death's untrodden realm.'" The phrase in the creed, "He descended into hell," is inserted to make it quite definite that he was in no trance-like state, but did really die and come back to men from *death*. Couldn't he have said one word, or brought one message from beyond the grave?

Well, he did. "Jesus met them, saying, All hail." The Greek word [10] may be translated "Rejoice!" It is a greeting, but it is also a report. It means "Rejoice! All is well!"

Further, when people say, "Shall I meet my loved ones again?" we may remember Jesus' word to the poor wretch on the cross next his own. "Today shalt thou be with me in paradise." If they did not recognize one another, there was small point in the meeting. Even if our loved ones died a long time ago, remember that "time" does not mean "age" in a timeless world.

"Age shall not weary them, nor the years condemn," and they will know and welcome us.

If we wonder at Jesus' silence, we may recall the Fourth Gospel, whose author could hardly have invented the words he ascribes to Jesus: "I go to prepare a place for you . . . , that where I am, there ye may be also." "And if it were not so, I would have told you." [11] Jesus was quite certain that all are living souls to God, whether alive on earth or in heaven, "for all live unto him." [12]

Yet our earnest gaze cannot penetrate very far, and a reverent attitude of "There is much I cannot know" must be accepted. "I have no idea what it will be like," said the late Dr. Temple to his wife, "and I think that I am glad that I have not, as I am sure it would be wrong." [13] The *fact* of life after death I am sure of. Its manner is bound to be uncertain for several reasons:

1. There are no categories of thought, no descriptive words which can give any true picture of a mode of life presumably quite different from our own. Why, we cannot even give a man born blind a description of a sunset; we are not able to convey to him what "seeing" means. We are talking about a faculty which he does not possess. Imagine try-

[10] χαίρετε.
[11] John 14.
[12] Luke 20:38.
[13] *Op. cit.*, p. 626.

ing to describe to a stone-deaf man, who had always been thus, the glory of a piece of grand music. You would have to tell the blind man that the sunset was like music and the deaf man that the music was like the sunset, and how far would either understand? Yet both blind and deaf have everything else in common with us. How could the dead possibly describe to us a life outside the body altogether, without any of the five senses, beyond time and beyond space? Imagination cannot bridge the gulf. By a stretch of imagination we can make a fanciful picture of the butterfly stooping to explain his new life to the caterpillar, or the gorgeous-winged dragonfly addressing the larva from which it springs. The only words to describe the new life—words like "air" and "height" and "flying"—mean nothing. It is better to admit a reverent agnosticism and say with Paul, "Eye hath not seen, nor ear heard, neither have entered into the heart of man, the things which God hath prepared for them that love him." [14]

2. There is perhaps another reason why Jesus veiled from man the glory beyond. Would it not make man intolerant of the limitations of this life to glimpse the other?

I remember college days well enough to recall how we all longed for the time when we should leave college. *Then* we should be free. Yet it was no good. We could not cut short the days, and to leave would mean to be unqualified and to renounce our dreams forever. I believe that the next life is so incredibly beautiful that any beauty, or love, or goodness we have glimpsed here is but a shadow compared with *that* reality. Would it be good for us to see it? Should we try to take a short cut and —in earth language—postpone our realization of the dream?

If we saw heaven, could we bear earth again? I feel that when at last I do see God, it must be forever. It is said that man has gradually emerged from a type of ape. I was at the zoo quite recently and saw in a cage a brooding chimpanzee. I felt very humble. But in my heart I said, "Brother, I'm glad I haven't to return to that stage. Life is pretty limited, but it's better than that!" But as monkey is to man, so is man to what he will become. "It doth not yet appear what we shall be," [15] but if we could guess what the highest heaven holds for man, we should never want to return to the cage of earth and the limitations of the flesh and space and time. Poor Lazarus! I wonder if he *did* have to come back from

[14] I Cor. 2:9.
[15] I John 3:2.

some splendid glory of which he got just a hint! Back to the cage of earth, back to a dirty little Jewish town, back to the daily round, back to Martha's tongue! If so, no wonder he was morose all the rest of his days, dreaming, waiting, longing.

3. It might not only be dissatisfying; it might be disintegrating. This human brain, these faculties, this shrouded life, this limited vision—these are for the earth life. Could the mind remain normal if the supernatural splendors of the other world suddenly burst upon it? I don't know. I have always thought it merciful that at the Transfiguration a cloud swept the mountain. Jesus was at home in both worlds, but Peter was not, nor James and John. Was it the mercy of God that they were so tired that they slept on the warm heather, and that "when they had lifted up their eyes, they saw no man, save Jesus *only*."

We must await the gentle schooling and preparation of Brother Death. I wish I could say two sentences to take away the fear of death from some gentle hearts.

First, remember that coming into *this* world would be terrifying if you could have thought about it, leaving the security and peace and warmth of the womb. And you cried like anything at the new phase of life. But God made a mother's love to receive you, and a mother's arms to infold you, and a mother's care to protect you. Don't you think you might trust God to supply all that you need when you pass into the next phase?

Second, for what it is worth, my evidence is that dying is a beautiful experience. Most people die in their sleep. Spasmodic movements of Brother Body, as he tries to hold back a man, do not represent an agony of mind. If people are conscious to the last, in my experience—and I have seen many people die—it is a wonderfully joyous affair.[16] They often will smile. After weeks during which they could not raise their heads for weakness they will sit up with radiant faces and call out the name of one they loved, though it be one who is long since dead. Professor William Hunter, the famous physician, on his deathbed said, "If I had strength to hold a pen, I would write how easy and pleasant a thing it is to die."

Accept that comfort, and,

[16] I have set out the evidence in *Why Do Men Suffer?* pp. 234 ff.

Sustained and soothed
By an unfaltering trust, approach thy grave,
Like one who wraps the drapery of his couch
About him, and lies down to pleasant dreams.[17]

Yet I do not think we ought to call death a sleep. Life on earth should be called a sleep—a sleep with many bad dreams and innumerable nightmares. It is death alone that is worthy of the word "awakening." Perhaps you will wake up in heaven on the morning after death and look back on the whole of your life as if it were a troubled dream. And those who welcome you may say what Shelley said about his dear dead Keats:

Peace, peace! he is not dead, he doth not sleep—
He hath awakened from the dream of life.

[17] William Cullen Bryant, "Thanatopsis."

XXI

Is Christianity Out of Date?

He is risen from the dead; and, behold, he goeth before you into Galilee; there shall ye see him. —Matt. 28:7

Why seek ye the living among the dead? —Luke 24:5

He made as though he would go further. —Luke 24:28 Revised Version

MANY PEOPLE ASK QUESTIONS WHICH SUGGEST THAT IN THEIR VIEW Christ has "had his day." "He lived so long ago," they say, "and in such different circumstances. His ideas were lovely, but they don't fit today. His religion belongs to the past."

It is a complete misunderstanding of Christianity to regard it merely as a religion established in the long-distant past and sending out its influence into the future. It would be more true to regard it as a religion of the future to which we have not yet attained. Christ beckons to us from the future. He does not merely wave to us from the past.

Of course, Christianity had its historical setting at a definite period in time and at a definite geographical place. Unlike other religions we could name, it is firmly established historically and geographically and does not run back into legend and myth when one traces its origin. But it is of immense importance that we should understand that Christ was not merely a historical person who moved across the stage of history, doing and saying beautiful things, setting mankind a wonderful example to follow, and then passing into the Great Silence. He is alive and always *going before us.*

Ruskin, in his *Modern Painters,* used to encourage people to read the Gospels imaginatively and, to use his own words, "to be present, as if in the body, at each recorded event in the life of the Redeemer." I recommend this to you. It is a most useful thing to picture Jesus standing on the beach of the blue Sea of Galilee, with earth's sunshine on his face and heaven's sunshine in his heart, teaching, healing, blessing little children, and so on. But we must do that only in order to help us translate all he stands for into the life of today, and see him a living Spirit moving in our world, in our circumstances, in our daily lives. Unless we do this, we shall attempt the futility of imprisoning him in a tomb called history. He will not stay in tombs. He always rises from the dead. He always goes before us. He is always making "as though he would go further."

Matthew Arnold, in "Obermann Once More," wrote:

> Now he is dead! Far hence he lies
> In the lorn Syrian town,
> And on his grave, with shining eyes,
> The Syrian stars look down.

The poetry is excellent, but this is not Christianity. Whittier speaks more truly when he says:

> No fable old, no mythic lore,
>   No dream of bards and seers,
> No dead fact stranded on the shore
>   Of the oblivious years;
>
> But warm, sweet, tender, even yet
>   A present help is he;
> And faith has still its Olivet,
>   And love its Galilee.

He *goeth before you* into Galilee, into that Galilee where you are now. Go back into history to assure yourself of the stability of the Christian faith, but use it only to interpret the living present. History is dead. "Why seek ye the living among the dead?" He is beckoning you from the future and always making "as though he would go further."

There is a slang phrase which, like many other slang phrases, is very eloquent. We speak of people "refusing to stay put." I should like to show you how typical that was of Jesus from the earliest days.

Let us imaginatively talk to some of the people who knew him best in those far-off years. When Jesus was twelve years of age, they took him up to the temple. It must have been a tremendously exciting adventure for him. Handel at twelve was a musical genius. Jesus at twelve was a religious genius. And to go up to the temple ceremonies at the feast must have been as exciting for him as it would be for the boy Handel to hear some great concert, or for our boys to be shown the engines of a modern airplane and to be taken for a thrilling flight. Off they went in two parties, the men traveling in one and the women in another. On the return journey, at the end of the first day, Jesus is missing. Let us ask Joseph what he thinks about it.

"Well," says Joseph, "of course he is a dear lad, but he is always giving us trouble. When we got to the end of the first day's journey home, I thought he was with Mary, and Mary thought he was with me, and we had to go all the way back to Jerusalem. And where do you think we found him? Sitting among the professors of theology and asking them questions—and the most extraordinary questions at that. Mary told him that we had been looking for him everywhere, and he just threw his arms round her neck and said, 'Surely you knew that I had to be about my Father's business.' I had to put an end to it and bring him home, but he didn't want to come. It was only his sense of loyalty to us that brought him home at all. He seemed to want to go on asking questions."

Yes, mentally and spiritually, even as a boy, "he made as though he would go further."

We turn to Mary and ask her. She loved him dearly, but she never understood him until, perhaps, when she stood by his cross. "What was he like?" we ask. "Oh!" she says. "He was a lovely boy, but of course he was a handful to look after. I would hear someone creeping about stealthily in the night, long before the dawn broke, and then I would watch him slipping out at the door, quietly so as not to waken anybody, and he would not be back until the sun was high in the sky and it was time for school or work. Suddenly I would see him appear in the doorway, his hair all tousled and wet with the dew, and I would say, 'Wherever have you been?' And he would say, 'Oh! Up in the hills with my Father.' He just would not stay put. The other children would sleep quietly all night and wake up and have their breakfast. But he loved to go out on the hills wandering about by himself, sitting for hours watching the sunrise and the colors in the sky and on the sea. You could never be quite sure what he was going to do next." Even as a boy "he made as though he would go further."

We turn to the rabbi at Nazareth and ask him if he remembers Jesus. "Remember him," he says. "I should think I do. He gave me some bad times. He was always wanting to have the copy of the Scriptures to look at, and, of course, the sacred rolls are kept under lock and key, and no one may have them without my permission. He was always badgering me to get at them, and continually asked me why I believed this, and why I believed that, and what Moses said about this, and what the Scriptures taught about that."

I imagine that the poor rabbi felt rather as Charles felt about Joan of Arc in Bernard Shaw's play, when Charles, nearly distracted, said, "Why doesn't she shut up or go home?" I think the rabbi at Nazareth must often have felt like that about Jesus. Mentally and spiritually Jesus always "made as though he would go further." He wouldn't shut up. He wouldn't stay put.

Let us turn to his brother James. "Well," says James, "frankly I found him very difficult, although I could bite my tongue out now on account of the angry things I said to him." (We remember how full James's epistle is of strong, fierce words about the dangers of the tongue.) "But really it was difficult. When our father Joseph died, Jesus had to carry on the business, and I wanted him to extend it. I wanted to go to Cana of Galilee, where my sister got married, and open a branch of our business there. But Jesus seemed to think that if we were making enough money to keep the family in moderate comfort, it was silly to want to extend it, since he wanted to be free from it altogether and start preaching what he called his good news of the kingdom. And at last, when he knew I was old enough to take the responsibility, he just downed tools and left me to it. Of course I could manage, but I knew we should never be wealthy as I wanted to be. Besides, if he *had* to go and preach, why didn't he become a rabbi in the proper manner and go to college, and take a degree, and then settle down in one of the villages and get to know the people, and do everything a rabbi ought to do? Instead of that he started to preach in such a way that they threw him out of the synagogue and nearly murdered him, and again and again he called the whole bench of bishops hypocrites. It made things very difficult for us in the village. Our local rabbi was frightfully angry. But Jesus just would not be conventional." No, always making "as though he would go further."

It is all very well for us to imagine that it would have been lovely to have been with Jesus in the days of his flesh. It is all very well for the children to sing that lovely hymn which includes the line "I should like to have been with them then."

But do let us realize that it was not all honey and sitting about on green grass and being fed and watching him heal and sharing his popularity. You may have noticed that even physically the disciples were so tired that, again and again, they fell asleep as soon as they sat down. On the Mountain of Transfiguration, for instance, their eyes were heavy, and in Gethsemane they were too worn out to share his agony. They repeatedly fell asleep.

Notice the significance of some of the sentences we read so glibly. "They departed to another village." "He crossed over to the other side." "He must needs go through Samaria." Why? Nobody else did. Every other Jewish traveler made a wide detour to avoid going through Samaria. The hostility between Jews and Samaritans was so fierce that you carried your life in your hands. But of course he *must* go through Samaria because that was like him. He had "not where to lay his head," we read, but that was not because he was poor. Jesus was not actually a very poor man. He did not wonder where the next meal was coming from. Judas kept a bag, and rich widows in Jerusalem kept it full. Jesus wore such beautiful clothes that his executioners were loath to cut them in pieces. They cast lots for them. He was not ragged and down-and-out; and as for a place to lay his head, hundreds of people would have given him a place and been proud to do it. What he means by the phrase is, "I must go further. I must always be on the move. My loins are girded, and my lamp is burning, and I am a traveler." "The foxes have holes;" that is to say, they have a base from which they operate and a place of refuge to which they constantly return. Similarly, "the birds of the air have nests; but the Son of man hath not where to lay his head." Divine compulsions move him on continually. "Other sheep I have, which are not of this fold: them also I *must* bring." "I *must* preach the kingdom of God to the other cities also: for therefore am I sent." "I *must* work the works of him that sent me, while it is day."

He teaches his men to live in the same way. They are not to take heavy luggage, not even a wallet, not even a spare pair of shoes for the rough, muddy roads. It is almost humorous to imagine their puzzled faces. "What! No wallet? No staff? No shoes? No spare cash? Can't we enjoy ourselves in the homes of our beneficent hosts?" No, they are to give their blessing on the house and then pass on. They are on the King's business, and the King's business demands haste.

We read the gospel record and realize that there is breathlessness behind it. Read the first chapter of Mark again, and you will notice how many times the word "straightway" occurs in the chapter. When we read the sentence, "In my Father's house are many mansions," we seem to breathe a sigh of relief and think it sounds like rest. But alas, the Greek word is "monai," and, having looked up the famous Dr. Westcott,[1] we find to our dismay that the word means "resting places or inns at the side of a road, where travellers find refreshment." Even death seems to mean just staying the night at an inn and then taking to the uphill road again, a road that ends beyond our vision in the high mountains of that perfection which is God's plan for every soul.

So even his grave is for Jesus only a two nights' lodging. "He wakens on Sunday morning and goes on, always making as though he would go further."

Now here is certainly a message for the modern church, the church that loves him but so constantly makes the mistake of trying to imprison him. He always breaks out of prisons. They become graves for him, and he does not like graves. He leaves them empty and moves on; and if we want to find him, we must move on also, or we shall be left behind, looking for the living among the dead. Walt Whitman's lines exactly express the challenge I want to make:

> We too take ship O soul,
> Joyous we too launch out on trackless seas,
> . . . .
> Caroling free, singing our song of God,
> Chanting our chant of pleasant exploration.
> . . . .
> Sail forth—steer for the deep waters only,
> Reckless O soul, exploring, I with thee, and thou with me,
> For we are bound where the mariner has not yet dared to go,
> And we will risk the ship, ourselves and all.
>
> O my brave soul!
> O farther farther sail!
> O daring joy, but safe! are they not all the seas of God?
> O farther, farther, farther sail!

1. Notice how we try to bury Jesus in *organization*. Don't tell me that organization is necessary. I know it. Every idea must have ex-

[1] *Commentary on the Gospel of St. John,* pp. 200-201.

pression in organization if the idea is to be of practical value. But how often is the slogan true in religion that when the idea has created the organization, the organization proceeds to kill the idea.

If you think I am unkind, take that church organization to which you are particularly attached and ask how long a stranger would have to attend it in order to find the living Christ. I don't mean anything mushy or sentimental. I don't mean anything visionary or mystical. I mean what I say. How long would a stranger have to come to your meetings before he felt, "Ah! There is alive in this organization the spirit of the living Christ. This organization is different from all secular organizations. It expresses the living Jesus"? How many organizations should we close down if we would have nothing to do with an organization that did not embody the living spirit of our Lord? Are we surprised that the passer-by passes by? People cannot be blamed for refusing to seek the living among the dead.

Six of our young people were accepted into membership of the City Temple recently, and we welcome them with our love and prayers. But I would say to them, "Be careful when they put you on a committee." By all means you must serve the church with all your powers, but do not get entangled in activities that will spoil the vision that burned in your heart when you were received into the church. For many shall say to Jesus in that day, "Lord, did we not serve on this committee and that, and did we not raise much money for your funds, and did we not hold every office open to a layman? Yes, and indeed, did we not enter the holy ministry?" And to many will he say in that day, "I never knew you. I had gone on before you, and you would not follow. You sought me, the living one, among dead organizations. Why sought ye the living among the dead? I am always going further, and if you want my transforming friendship, you must be prepared to travel."

2. Notice how we try to bury Jesus in *words*. I am not making any cheap jibe against creeds. I want only to remind you why the creeds were written at all. They were not written down by men who believed that they were the final form which Christianity should take. They were written to rebut error. They were written to combat attack. They embodied all that the Christian religion meant to the men who wrote them down. We must respect them and honor them. But I am glad I am a Free Churchman and need not repeat them. They no longer

embody the living spirit of Christ. In old-fashioned language they labor to state truths which can be expressed far less ambiguously. They were once the verbal clothes of Christ, but his graveclothes remained in his tomb, and he clothed himself afresh when he moved further. I wish we could restate our belief afresh every ten years and press into our service new thought forms, new ways of apprehending reality. Instead of that we mumble words often after the life and meaning have passed away from them and try to make ourselves believe by repeating dead formulas. It's no good going into tombs and paying too much regard to empty graveclothes. He is not there! He is risen! Why seek ye the living among the dead?

Do not let us think that the Free Churches are free from all blame, for consider the absurdities in some of our hymns. Let us realize that if a tune is well known, it is sung lustily by large congregations who give little or no thought to the silly sentimentalities and the meaningless phrases that they are using. Recently in a group of Christian people who had sung the hymn containing the line "Here I raise mine Ebenezer" I took the liberty of asking how many people knew what the line meant. Not one of them had the faintest idea of the Old Testament story lying behind the phrasing. Without such knowledge the words of course are meaningless mumbo jumbo.

I am sympathetic with all who love ceremony and ritual and tradition, but I would scrap everything that does not bring the soul to the reality of the living Christ. I would have done with dead forms that mean nothing. He does not wave to us from the past; he beckons us from the future. The best verse in a well-known hymn sounds the note we want here:

Crown Him the Lord of Truth,
The past He leaves behind,
And reigns in His eternal youth
And rules the honest mind.

3. Notice how we try to bury Jesus in past *experiences*. I must speak here tenderly and gently, and that is what I wish to do. But let me ask if twenty, thirty, even forty years ago, you had a wonderful experience of religion. You heard a message, or read a book, or walked alone, perhaps, under the quiet stars and made a pact with Christ. You gave him your young manhood or womanhood. You were quite sincere.

You knew the reality of his presence, and perhaps for weeks you walked on air. Is it unkind to say that now, in the garden of your heart, there is an empty tomb? You don't meet him now in that garden, for he has gone on. It is a garden of remembrance where there are graves but no refreshing meetings with our Lord. You say that twenty years ago you gave your heart to Christ. Splendid! But you cannot treasure that experience and live on it forever. He has gone on before you, and you must make haste and catch up with him, for he is beckoning you to new experiences and new spiritual adventures and new tasks and new revelations of himself and new meanings of life, new reserves of power and new depths of serenity.

Years ago when I was a boy I attended with my father and mother a most thrilling display of magic by Maskelyne and Cook, as they were then called. One of the items was called "The Artist's Dream." When the curtain went up, the artist, who had recently lost his wife, was painting a portrait of her sitting in a swing in a lovely garden. Then he seated himself near the foot of the easel and fell asleep. As he slept, the woman in the picture stepped down from the easel, bent over her husband, put her hand on his shoulder, and spoke to him. You could see the empty swing. Then she returned into the picture. The artist wakened, went to the picture, and lifted it down in front of the audience. It was only a picture.

I have not, of course, the least idea of how it was all done, but it became a parable I have never forgotten. Is Christ to you a beautiful picture in a frame called history, or does he, in some moment of quiet devotion, move out of the picture and become a living friend?

Let me imagine a woman who has lost her husband and is sad of heart. She carries on his work. That is to say she engages in the *organization* which he initiated. But is that enough? She reads over and over again his love letters. But are his beautiful *words* enough? She gazes at his portrait and treasures the tender memories of past *experiences* when they were lovers together in the past. But is that enough? Organization, words, experiences. . . . "No!" she cries, with passionate sorrow in her voice, "I want *him!*"

But alas! she cannot have him. On that mystery I will not now dwell. But Jesus she *can* have. Indeed, the central fact of Christianity is that he is alive and available and present. Don't be content with organizations or words or memories. Don't look back to Jesus as though he lived only in the past. He is no longer in the grave of that "lorn Syrian town." He is risen. He goes before you. He beckons you to follow him. His spirit calls to your own, making "as though he would go further," and waiting for your response.

> We too take ship O soul,
> Joyous we too launch out on trackless seas.
> . . . .
> O my brave soul!
> O farther farther sail!
> O daring joy, but safe! are they not all the seas of God?
> O farther, farther, farther sail!

"He made as though he would go further." Who will follow him?